Palgrave Studies in Islamic Banking, Finance, and Economics

Series Editors
Mehmet Asutay, Business School, Durham University, Durham, UK
Zamir Iqbal, Islamic Development Bank, Jeddah, Saudi Arabia
Jahangir Sultan, Bentley University, Boston, MA, USA

The aim of this series is to explore the various disciplines and sub-disciplines of Islamic banking, finance and economics through the lens of theoretical, practical, and empirical research. Monographs and edited collections in this series will focus on key developments in the Islamic financial industry as well as relevant contributions made to moral economy, innovations in instruments, regulatory and supervisory issues, risk management, insurance, and asset management. The scope of these books will set this series apart from the competition by offering in-depth critical analyses of conceptual, institutional, operational, and instrumental aspects of this emerging field. This series is expected to attract focused theoretical studies, in-depth surveys of current practices, trends, and standards, and cutting-edge empirical research.

Ahmet Suayb Gundogdu

Food Security, Affordable Housing, and Poverty

An Islamic Finance Perspective

Ahmet Suayb Gundogdu
Istanbul Sabahattin Zaim University
Istanbul, Turkey

ISSN 2662-5121   ISSN 2662-513X (electronic)
Palgrave Studies in Islamic Banking, Finance, and Economics
ISBN 978-3-031-27688-0   ISBN 978-3-031-27689-7 (eBook)
https://doi.org/10.1007/978-3-031-27689-7

© The Editor(s) (if applicable) and The Author(s), under exclusive license to Springer Nature Switzerland AG 2023
This work is subject to copyright. All rights are solely and exclusively licensed by the Publisher, whether the whole or part of the material is concerned, specifically the rights of translation, reprinting, reuse of illustrations, recitation, broadcasting, reproduction on microfilms or in any other physical way, and transmission or information storage and retrieval, electronic adaptation, computer software, or by similar or dissimilar methodology now known or hereafter developed.
The use of general descriptive names, registered names, trademarks, service marks, etc. in this publication does not imply, even in the absence of a specific statement, that such names are exempt from the relevant protective laws and regulations and therefore free for general use.
The publisher, the authors, and the editors are safe to assume that the advice and information in this book are believed to be true and accurate at the date of publication. Neither the publisher nor the authors or the editors give a warranty, expressed or implied, with respect to the material contained herein or for any errors or omissions that may have been made. The publisher remains neutral with regard to jurisdictional claims in published maps and institutional affiliations.

This Palgrave Macmillan imprint is published by the registered company Springer Nature Switzerland AG
The registered company address is: Gewerbestrasse 11, 6330 Cham, Switzerland

Ahmet Suayb Gundogdu

There are some who impress you with their views regarding worldly affairs and openly call upon Allah to witness what is in their hearts, yet they are your worst adversaries. And when they leave, they strive throughout the land to spread mischief in it and destroy crops and cattle. Allah does not like mischief.

- 2:204–205 -

Preface

There is a tendency in conventional economics and finance academia to be apologetic when dealing with globally prevailing unfair economic and financial systems. This makes poverty inevitable, no matter the technological development of a country. The Islamic economics and finance academia is not immune from this tendency. This book is the product of an attempt to look differently at the issue of poverty intermingled with food security and affordable housing. The book aims to raise awareness about the root causes and suggests novel proposals that will lead to sustainable solutions. It is based on the understanding that if we continue doing more of the same things, we cannot expect to produce different results. The book is also premised on the understanding that the financial sector can promote economic progress only if it channels capital to the most productive use while avoiding moral hazard and adverse selection. The issue of collateral taking promotes a situation where financial institutions prefer to lend only to-big-to-fail structures for shelter and food sectors that fuel poverty and inequality. The conduct of financial institutions promotes real estate hoarding, which impedes providing affordable shelter to the young generation. In agriculture, it promotes lending to big agricultural producers and overlooks smallholder farmers. This adverse selection ultimately gives rise to food security and affordable housing issues. This indicates that financial liberalization is not the solution to dealing with poverty and inequality. Instead, strong policy stands and financial regulations to direct capital to provide long-term sustainability are needed.

Both food and shelter are underpinnings of poverty per the Islamic definition of poverty. These two subjects have a strong resemblance. The food and shelter problem has remarkably similar root causes related to policy discourse and the use of harmful financing.

Regarding the issue of shelter in the development arena, the discussion revolves around affordability. We still have not solved the shelter problem despite massive technological development. This is because affordability prevents us from taking advantage of cost-effective construction novelties. Today, building shelters would have been much cheaper if the financial policies did not fuel a rise in land and house prices. For instance, providing mortgages with long tenors to finished houses increases the number of bidders, and the general public pays more than the shelter should cost. The same mechanism increases land prices. One solution for this challenge is to impose land use policies, such as a time limit for ownership and Zakat on land purchased for hoarding and speculation. Such policies would impede the hoarding of urban and rural land. Another approach to tackling food security and shelter would be using finance on the production side. Financing trading of finished houses and agricultural commodities fuels prices, leading to increased bidding. Hence, the remedy for the challenge of unaffordable housing and lack of food security is the same: Zakat-based management of land use policy.

Can we solve the problem of unaffordable housing and lack of food security if we stop tunneling financial resources to purchases? Unfortunately, the case is a bit more convoluted. Bringing future demand forward, with debt-creating Islamic finance contracts such as Murabaha, to boost the economy is an accepted concept as long as such demand does not give rise to unfair price formation/hike. Financing should be channeled for both production and consumption without distorting prices. Proper Islamic lending contracts should be harnessed with matching resource mobilization/securitization contracts to avoid systematic risk for the financial sector and assure fair price formation for the public. A mismatch between lending and resource mobilization/securitization markets is the general characteristic of financial crises.

Islamic perspective on food and shelter revolves around fair price formation to assure affordability and healthy supply and demand of food and shelter. On the one hand, we need to ensure supply by production. On the other hand, we should ensure that there is matching demand created with debt contracts while assuring unfair exploitive price formation. These two areas are essential to tackle poverty alleviation, which is still at the top of the development agenda, regardless of many decades of development efforts. Unlike things that may look like for non-experts, the housing case is easier to resolve by policy discourse to limit the time of land ownership and impose Zakat on land hoarders. As it is, the land is purchased for infinity in many jurisdictions, and such a time dimension yields skyrocketing asset price calculations unrelated to the cost of production. By limiting the period of land ownership, we can assure affordability. Hence, the first chapter will present the details and Islamic opposition to rent control as an alternative. The chapter also discusses the systematic risk created to the financial and economic system by the real estate sector. The second chapter presents a supply-side intervention with mortgages and securitization with Islamic finance tools.

In the subsequent chapters, the issue of food security is discussed from an Islamic perspective. The third chapter identifies the root cause of food insecurity as unfair price formation in the agricultural input and output markets, mainly due to financial derivatives. Today, the majority of food in the world is produced in a relatively small area with massive irrigation. These economies of scale do not allow smallholder farmers to have a more resilient and competitive supply market. Any climate issue in these mass production areas would lead to supply shortages, even if a handful of agricultural commodity producers do not take advantage of their dominant position to impose higher prices. Even without natural hazard risk to such mass scale agricultural commodity production business model, it is not wise to leave the world population at the mercy of a few agricultural commodity producers. Hence, the fourth chapter is dedicated to creating an enabling environment with Islamic finance intervention to address the issue of trading agricultural commodities for smallholder farmers. Financial derivatives mainly contribute to price fluctuation in agricultural input and output markets. Hence, they are the main contributor to food insecurity. In this chapter, Islamic alternatives such as asset-backed Murabaha with a margin call and Islamic future contract are introduced to guarantee market price stability and supply predictable prices for food processors. Addressing the demand side market structure alone would not suffice to stabilize agricultural commodity prices. Hence, the fifth chapter is dedicated to a case of financing cotton production, a cash crop, by smallholder farmers under an agricultural cooperative.

For housing and food security, with proper Islamic finance intervention, we can stabilize prices, and assure steady production of assets, and healthy demand without increasing prices, hence eradicating poverty. This aspect of supply and demand is similar for both shelter and food. Another similarity for both food and shelter problem is enabling economic and social infrastructure for rural and urban settings. Chapter 6 elaborates on the Islamic perspective of the provision of enabling infrastructures. Again, the focus on infrastructure development is availability while ignoring affordability and long-term sustainability. The chapter identifies the best business model for providing economic and social infrastructure for rural and urban areas to assure affordability and sustainability. Chapter 7 elaborates on the role of government and has concluding remarks on the importance of Taqwa (Islamic DOs and DON'Ts) to achieve Pareto optimal solutions and the use of finance subjects for the more significant benefit of society rather than individual enrichment. Accordingly, Taqwa's approach to affordable housing and food security in pursuit of poverty alleviation is provided.

Istanbul, Turkey   Ahmet Suayb Gundogdu

Contents

1 **Affordable Housing and Poverty** 1
   The Role of Price Formation and Land Use Policy 6
   The Role of Zakat 10
   Zakat from Company Shareholding 16
   The Role of Waqf 19
   State Housing Development Projects 24
   References 25

2 **Islamic Mortgages and Securitization** 27
   The Issue of Resource Mobilization and Securitization 28
     Bai Al-Inah 33
     Bai Al-Dayn (Islamic Discounting/Factoring) 33
     Organized Tawarruq: Commodity Murabaha 34
   Islamic Mortgages and Lending 36
     Murabaha as Practiced by Islamic Banks for House Financing 38
     Ijara as Practiced by Islamic Banks House Financing 40
   Islamic Resource Mobilization 42
     Ethis Crowdfunding, Indonesia 43
     Islamic Rent-Supporter Lottery System, Turkey 47
   The Next Level Housing Program 48
     The Role of Community Waqf in Real Estate Development 53
   References 54

xiii

3 Food Security and Poverty 57
SDGs and Food Security 61
Fi'sabilillah Spending 65
Zakat for Poverty Alleviation and Food Security 67
Economic Empowerment Programs 70
The Issue of Agricultural Prices 74
Post-Harvest Losses and the Role of Warehousing 79
International Trade of Agricultural Commodities 80
References 82

4 Financing the Trade of Agricultural Commodities 87
Islamic Trade Finance Contracts and Risk for Financiers 88
   Risk in Asset-Based Islamic Trade Finance Contracts 88
   Risk in Asset-Backed Islamic Trade Finance Contracts 93
Margin Call 107
   Murabaha Sale: Asset-Based or Asset-Backed 107
   Commodity Price Risk Management 111
Islamic Future Contract and Liquidity Management 119
   Shari'ah Non-compliant Products on the Stage 120
   Shari'ah Compliant Alternatives from the Grassroots 120
References 123

5 Financing the Production of Agricultural Commodities 125
Cotton Cooperative and Financing 127
What is Structured Trade Finance 130
   Financing Based on Warehouse Receipt 131
   Financing Based on Export Receivable 131
Financing Facility Structure 132
Financier's Security Structure 133
   Schedule of Implementation and Security Package 134
   Collateral Management 138
Assessment of the Structure 140
Annex-I Export Cash Flow 143
Annex-II Salam Price Calculation 143
References 145

6 Enabling Infrastructure 147
Definition and Categorization of Infrastructure 151
Sustainability Parameters 155
Business Model for Service Delivery 157

	Contracts for Asset Development	160
	Resource Mobilization to Scale-up	165
	References	170
7	**The Role of the State**	173
	Hisbah	174
	Infrastructure: Output, Outcome, and Services	175
	Determinants of Success	177
	References	180
Index		181

List of Figures

Fig. 2.1	Resource mobilization/securitization and lending (*Source* Author)	30
Fig. 2.2	Organized *Tawarruq* with commodity *Murabaha*. (*Source* Gundogdu [2014])	35
Fig. 2.3	Phase 1, Istisna contract for construction (*Source* Ethis crowdfunding)	45
Fig. 2.4	Phase 2, Murabaha contract for the sale of finished houses (*Source* Ethis Crowdfund	46
Fig. 2.5	Rent-supporter lottery system (*Source* EminEvim)	48
Fig. 3.1	Commodity food price index (*Source* Index Mundi)	74
Fig. 3.2	Cotton monthly price—US dollars per kilogram (*Source* Index Mundi)	76
Fig. 4.1	Islamic trade finance contracts categorized (*Source* Gundogdu [2016a])	89
Fig. 4.2	Risk in asset-based *Murabaha* (*Source* Gundogdu [2016a])	90
Fig. 4.3	Transaction flow for asset-based Islamic export financing (*Source* Gundogdu [2016b])	92
Fig. 4.4	Transaction scheme of asset-backed *Murabaha* (*Source* Gundogdu [2016a])	94
Fig. 4.5	Risk in asset-backed *Murabaha* (*Source* Gundogdu [2016a])	96
Fig. 4.6	Schematic flow of the transaction (*Source* Gundogdu [2014])	109
Fig. 4.7	Sugar price volatility (*Source* Gundogdu [2014])	112

Fig. 4.8	Histogram for one-month sugar price change (*Source* Gundogdu [2014])	114
Fig. 4.9	Rank and percentile for six-month sugar price changes (*Source* Gundogdu [2014])	115
Fig. 4.10	Liquidity management based on asset-backed *Murabaha* through physical commodities in licensed warehouses (*Source* The author)	121
Fig. 6.1	Unlocking energy access finance through crowdfunding (*Source* Diallo and Gundogdu [2021])	166

List of Tables

Table 1.1	Outcome and output table as-is case; conventional approach	5
Table 1.2	Outcome and output table to-be case; Islamic approach	6
Table 1.3	Discouraging hoarding of land	14
Table 1.4	Company valuation methods	18
Table 2.1	Matching lending and resource mobilization	49
Table 3.1	The Millennium Development Goals (MDGs)	61
Table 3.2	Sustainable Development Goals (SDGs)	62
Table 3.3	Causes and solutions	64
Table 3.4	Classic microfinance vs. Islamic microfinance based on the economic empowerment concept	73
Table 4.1	Risk management in Islamic asset-based import financing	91
Table 4.2	Risk management in Islamic asset-based export financing	93
Table 4.3	Eligibility criteria for the obligor	97
Table 4.4	Eligibility criteria/responsibility for the collateral manager	98
Table 4.5	Assignment of receivable	100
Table 4.6	Descriptive Statistics for one-month sugar price change	112
Table 4.7	Descriptive statistics, security coverage, and cash deposit needed for 3–6–9 month's tenor financing	114
Table 4.8	Margin Call Illustration for six-month tenor financing	116
Table 5.1	Schedule of cotton financing cycle	135
Table 6.1	Infrastructure categorization	152
Table 6.2	Infrastructure subsectors	154
Table 6.3	Sustainability parameters	157
Table 7.1	Infrastructure sectors	176

Table 7.2	The role of government in Islam	177
Table 7.3	Lending and resource mobilization contract	178
Table 7.4	Discouraging hoarding of land	179

CHAPTER 1

Affordable Housing and Poverty

"The root causes of the problem in accessing affordable housing"

In Islam, paying Zakat, avoiding Riba, and spending to avoid hoarding have much more value than abstaining from fornication, theft, and drinking. The hoarding issue has not been appropriately preached since Al-Ahbari has been hoarding.[1] The importance, as well as the proper imposition of Zakat, is also ignored. Case Box 1.1 showcases the clarification from Muhammad (ﷺ).

> **Case Box 1.1: The merit of Paying Zakat**
> I went out one night (and found) the Messenger of Allah (ﷺ) walking all alone. There was no man with him. I thought that he did not like anyone walking along with him. So I began to walk in the light of the moon. He, however, turned his attention to me, saw me, and said: Who is this? I said: It is Abu Dharr. Let Allah make me a ransom for you. He said: Abu Dharr, come on. He (Abu Dharr) said: So I walked along with him for some time, and he said: The wealthy persons would have little (reward) on the Day of Resurrection, except upon whom Allah conferred goodness (wealth). He dispensed it to his right, left, in front of him, and at his back (just as the wind diffuses fragrance) and did good with it (riches). I went

---

[1] Referring to Shurah At Touba, Ayah 34 for الأخبار.

© The Author(s), under exclusive license to Springer Nature Switzerland AG 2023
A. S. Gundogdu, *Food Security, Affordable Housing, and Poverty*, Palgrave Studies in Islamic Banking, Finance, and Economics, https://doi.org/10.1007/978-3-031-27689-7_1

> along with him for some time when He said: Sit here. And he made me sit at a safe place, and there were stones around it, and he said to me: Sit here till I come to you. He went away on the stony ground till I could not see him. He stayed away from me, and he prolonged his stay. Then I heard him as he came back, and he was saying: Even if he committed theft and even if he committed fornication. When he came, I could not help asking him: Apostle of Allah, let Allah make me ransom for you; who were you speaking on the stony ground? I heard nobody is responding to you. He (the Holy Prophet) said: It was Gabriel who met me by the side of the stony ground and said: Give glad tidings to your Ummah that he who died without associating ought to with Allah would go into Paradise. I said: Gabriel, even if he committed theft and fornication? He said: Yes. I said: Even if he committed theft and fornication? He said: Yes; I again said: Even if he committed theft and fornication? He said: Yes, even if he drank wine
> *Source* Sahih Muslim, 2175

The religion of Islam advises a delicate balance by encouraging property ownership until a certain hoarding level, spending money on the first family, and then giving alms to the community. Discouraging hoarding, encouraging spending, and almsgiving are perceived as solutions to grapple with poverty. In Islam, poverty is one of the most important issues, which needs to be handled to the extent that it is similar to struggles against disbelief (kufr). Muhammad (ﷺ) said: "O Allah! I seek refuge from disbelief (kufr) and poverty."[2]

The definition of poverty in Islam is based on Zakat liability. A person is deemed poor if their net worth is negative. Unlike the conventional understanding of income, in Islam, a person should have shelter, a transport vehicle, and a certain amount of savings to ensure the affordability of needs for a year to be considered not poor. A person with a negative net worth is still deemed poor in Islam, even if they can generate a steady income. Today, such a steady income can be generated with debt bubbles. Hence, the Islamic view rejects any reference to the International Poverty Line based on income less than a certain amount a day that international organizations use as a reference.

[2] Sunan an-Nasa'i 5485.

The sound understanding of Zakat is linked to a comprehensive understating of the term hoarding. The Arabic term Ihtikar is used for collecting, doing wrong, and greediness. The word is mainly used when referring to people who buy more food than they need to sell at higher prices during times of shortage (Madni, 2013). There is a clear hadith: "He who hoards is a sinner."[3]

Even though it has generally been associated with food, hoarding applies to other basic human needs, including real estate. Hoarding works against fair price formation, which is the pivot of Islamic economics and finance. This is why state intervention is necessary (Gundogdu, 2019a, 2019b). The definition of hoarding reveals a delicate balance between Islamic encouragements of property ownership versus price distortion in the market. For example, a person who uses the property for utility and commercial purposes is not a hoarder. A person should pay Zakat on hoarded assets, including money. Avoiding Zakat payment is not a joke in Islamic belief, as indicated in Case Box 1.2.

> **Case Box 1.2: Hoarding of Money**
> Ahnaf B. Qais reported: While I was in the company of the (elites) of Quraish, Abu Dharr came there, and he was saying: Give glad tidings to the hoarders of riches that their backs would be branded (so deeply) that (the hot Iron) would come out of their sides, and when the backs of their necks would be branded, it would come out of their foreheads. He (Abu Dharr) then went away and sat down. I asked who he was. They said: He is Abu Dharr. I went to him and said: What is this that I heard from you which you were saying before? He said: I said nothing but only that which I heard from their Prophet (ﷺ). I again said: What do you say about this gift? He said: Take it, for today it is a benefit. But when it becomes a price for your religion, then abandon it
> *Source* Sahih Muslim, 2177

The problem of poverty, as conventionally defined, can supposedly be resolved with loans by stimulating economic growth. However, this solution often back fires in the long term. The conventional method of Riba loans without checks and balances only fuels poverty. Should poverty be defined in the Islamic way based on debt accumulation for higher real

---

[3] Sahih Muslim, 1605.

estate prices leading to negative net worth? The conventional economics argument about linking economic growth with income is irrelevant as poverty is defined based on net worth in Islam. The Islamic definition of poverty suggests that developed countries are not far ahead of the least developed countries regarding poverty statistics.

Given the definition, the Islamic understanding of poverty prioritizes affordable housing because providing housing is an important element of the poverty definition. Accomplishing this universal provision of affordable housing with reasonable prices will help avoid negative net worth, which creates poor people as defined in Islam. Islam accepts the concept of debt, but such debt should not lead to unfair price formation of real estate prices. A mortgage is a legal instrument by which the creditor receives the pledge of the debtor's residence as collateral. In practice, however, it was challenging to evict people from their homes due to the bias of courts and policymakers against lenders due to social repercussions. The financial sector pushed for strong foreclosure laws imposed on developing the secondary market to channel more funds to housing finance (Van Order, 2003). The debt-driven housing market yielded overdeveloped beautiful urban and suburban dwellings, yet unhappy people as the established system worked for capital owners against households.

Islamic mortgages cannot be different from conventional ones as the more conventional finance engages tangible assets, the more the nature of business resembles Islamic Finance. Yet, there should be a significant difference between Islamic finance contracts: late payment charges. In real life, however, Islamic banks often impose late payment charges similarly to conventional banks. Shari'ah scholars argue that late payment charges are permissible to avoid a moral hazard by borrowers, given that banks cannot accrue any benefit from late payment. This is a challenge to develop a secondary market for Islamic mortgages.

The issue of resource mobilization is an important topic given that the 2008 financial crisis emerged out of innovative resource mobilization/securitization products. Resorting conventional or Islamic deposit banks has a significant disadvantage related to the maturity mismatch, between deposits and loans, precipitating systematic financial sector risk. Once unaffordable, prices would sky-dive due to the liquidity crisis that emerged in the financial sector out of the mismatch. In this regard, alternatives might be looked for within the capital markets. The Sukuk for securitizing the mortgage loan is a potential method, yet there are serious Shari'ah compliance issues with the Sukuk, as-is many are based on: Bai

Table 1.1 Outcome and output table as-is case; conventional approach

Policy tool	Output	Outcome
Channel more funds with the lower interest rates for construction and purchase of houses	Produce more houses	Unaffordable housing

Source The author

Al-Dayn, Organized Tawarruq, and Bai Al-Inah. Such practices are not different from conventional instruments. It is unjustified to claim that Islamic banks as they are can help in facilitating the provision of affordable housing. The issue is more related to the policy aspect: availing more financing, being Islamic or conventional, to home purchases inflates house prices. The more funds are available and the lesser the interest rate, the more people bid for the finished houses. As it is practiced today, availing of more loans is not a solution. It is a root cause of unaffordability. The fundamentals of the mortgage and securitization topic will be discussed more in depth in the next chapter.

Table 1.1 indicates the outcome and output design of the present financial and economic system. It is assumed that affordable housing will be facilitated by producing more houses and availing more mortgages, assuming a trickle-down effect. However, channeling funds to the production and sale of houses gives rise to high land prices. Funneling more funds would increase land and house prices and undermine affordability. Besides, the financial sector will get exposed to assets that are not easy to liquidate in case of liquidity crunches. These recurring bubbles and crunches will continue due to the fundamentals of the present monetary system. Table 1.2 presents the Islamic approach.

The policy outcome should be to provide affordable shelter for all, so more houses should be built. To achieve the desired outcome with the targeted output, more houses should be produced while decreasing land and house prices. This chapter discusses the policy tool: "Decrease Land and House Prices." The next chapter elaborates on producing more houses by "channeling more funds with a lower markup to construction and purchase houses with Islamic finance."

Table 1.2 Outcome and output table to-be case; Islamic approach

Policy tool	Output	Outcome
– Channel more funds with a lower markup to construction and purchasing houses with Islamic finance – Decrease land and house prices by limiting land ownership time and Zakat on land/house hoarding	Produce more houses	Affordable Housing

Source The author

THE ROLE OF PRICE FORMATION AND LAND USE POLICY

Traditionally, it is argued that land prices are a combination of practical and social matters. There are supposedly four important determinants impacting land prices: population density, the desirability of land, suitability for development, and planning restriction (Egan, 1996). The saleability factors, as defined by Egan, are listed below (1996):

- **Location**: a convenient house with access to public transportation, schools, hospitals, shops, and recreational centers.
- **Condition**: a house with substantial expenses is less likely to be sold.
- **Type of Property**: in some countries, certain types of houses are more desired.
- **Specific Facilities**: large kitchen, garage, garden, heating features.
- **The appearance of the property**.
- **Local Planning Permission**: local development plan impacts the saleability of houses. For instance, a factory project nearby may have adverse effects, while access to supermarkets or transport networks may have positive effects.

The motivation of private entrepreneurship, which is acceptable and advised from an Islamic point of view, in housing is to increase the saleability and profit margins. On the other hand, to the finance expert, the major impediment to affordable housing is high land prices that get higher in the low interest rate environment (Gundogdu, 2019a, 2019b). Encouraging private entrepreneurship does not mean acceptance of unfair price formation by Islam. It is the other way around; the Islamic proposition is to produce assets efficiently, ensure the sustainability of assets, and affordable prices. Affordable price is only attainable with fair land prices. Skyrocketing land prices are guaranteed due to the Net Present Value calculation as long as there is no time limit for land ownership. It was the book entitled "*Theory of Investment Value*" by William (1938) that inspired asset valuation based on interest rates in the "Dividend Discount Model." William's (1938) formula for Net Present Value calculation:

$$NPV = \sum_{t=0}^{T} \frac{C_t}{(1+r)^t} \quad (1.1)$$

C = Cash flow at the time (t).
r = Discount rate expressed as a decimal.
t = Time.

would turn into

$$NPV = \frac{C}{r} \quad (1.2)$$

in the case of perpetuity (Gordon & Shapiro, 1956). The land component of the house would turn into a monopoly price setting.

For instance, if a house brings about $10,000 in rent a year, under a 4% p.a. interest environment, the house price would be $250,000. If the interest rate goes down to 2%, the house price would be predicted as $500,000 and $1,000,000 in the case of a 1% interest rate. Indeed, the case would even turn worse in case of inflation higher than the interest rate: a negative real interest rate environment without assuming the growth factor of rents. If we restrict land ownership to 99 years in a 1% interest rate environment, the Net Present Value would be around $626K. The predicted house price would be $429K and $244K in the case of 2% and 4% interest rates. In the case of zero interest rate, the Present Value calculation would go to infinity should we not limit the ownership duration. In the case of a 99-year ownership duration, the Present Value prediction of the house price is capped at $990K under zero interest rate.

Not surprisingly, the effect of interest rates on real estate prices is a well-established fact (Chiquier & Lea, 2009). The factor implies real estate appraisal as well. Under a declining interest rate environment, the appraiser would keep marking ever-increasing real estate valuations. The main reason behind this is the use of market value, defined based on the amount for which real estate can be exchanged on the appraisal date. That is a bigger ticket size of mortgage loans, more indebted households, and less affordability. The established codes for the independence of appraisers from both lender and borrower are not the remedy. The improved version of Mortgage Lending Value is a concept based on value-at-risk and recognized by the Basel I accord (Merril, 2009). Nevertheless, Mortgage Lending Value cannot smoothen the effect of interest rates on real estate prices. The sharp increase in interest rates can easily wipe out house prices and give rise to a financial crisis.

Indeed, there are three ways that are not suitable under the pretext of a conventional free economy in terms of addressing the high price issue:

i. Suppressing Periodic Payment (Pmt): limiting rent on housing.
ii. Limiting the time of land ownership to change the formula, which would predict the trend in asset prices based on the return generated.
iii. Imposing Zakat on hoarded houses based on the market value, noting that house prices are not separable from land prices. Hence, the subject of Zakat should be real estate hoarded.

Today, economic and financial policies, let alone decrease fuel house prices, substantially contribute to poverty as defined by the Islamic understanding. Central banks keep interest rates low to keep financial markets afloat, and land monopoly is defended in the name of freedom. Indeed, both supporting financial markets with low interest rates and unlimited land ownership bring about rent-seeking, which is marketed as freedom. The so-called alternative communism was also noted, but it can be described as an animal farm with tight control and oppression of the masses (Orwell, 1945). It is not hard to deduce that the so-called freedom, capitalism, and communism are massive exploitation of the masses by a few elites.

The Islamic proposition is much different, and wisdom is derived from the Quran:

> There are some who impress you with their views regarding worldly affairs and openly call upon Allah to witness what is in their hearts, yet they are your worst adversaries. And when they leave, they strive throughout the

land to spread mischief in it and destroy crops and cattle. Allah does not like mischief.

—2:204–205

Many verses in the Quran acknowledge the right of ownership of rural and urban property and the inheritance of these assets. On the other hand, fair price formation is at the heart of Islam, as monopolistic/oligopolistic price setting and price ceilings (*Narh*) is forbidden (Gundogdu, 2019a, 2019b). Putting ceilings on rent violates *Narh* principle while allowing land ownership without a time limit violates the Islamic principles related to monopolistic/oligopolistic price setting. Both unlimited time ownership of land and rent ceilings are not welcomed in Islamic economics.

The main focus of Islamic economics is fair price formulation. The price distortion due to government intervention or monopolistic/oligopolistic markets is unacceptable. As a result, limiting the rent prices or rent increase rates by the government is not acceptable in Islam. On the other hand, it is a must to impede unfair price formation due to monopolistic/oligopolistic markets. As a result, Islamic principles necessitate time limits on land ownership to avoid land hoarding by a tiny minority that can and will have the absolute liberty of imposing prices. An Islamic solution can be, not to impose rent ceilings, but to limit land ownership to 99 Hijri years.

This policy would:

- Discourage rent-seeking in society, making society more dynamic. This policy would urge parents to better arm their kids with relevant education rather than accumulating land for sustenance.
- Directing landowners to resort to trade and production rather than rent-seeking for themselves and their children.

Ownership and inheritance rights are well acknowledged in the Quran as ways to make the land productive. Limiting land ownership time to 99 Hijri years would make the land more productive while fulfilling fair price realization in the market by impeding monopolistic/oligopolistic price setting. Since there would be no hoarding of idle land, people would have access to land for production.

So far, our discussion has been related to urban real estate. Rural land is slightly different due to the peculiarities of pastoral agricultural use.

In the case of rural land, land ownership should be also limited. Still, it should be assured that the land is transferred to people in the same region to ensure local farming knowledge is transferred from generation to generation. Priority should be given to the progeny of farmer-owners. The importance of local farming knowledge is key to food security, as discussed in Chapter 3. The only sustainable way for food security is to rely on smallholder farmers to cultivate all global land as opposed to the as-is approach of relying on a small part of the global land for much of global food production.

The Role of Zakat

A policy direction that channels funds with low markup would create housing price bubbles that would later burst and harm many, including the financial sector. The remedy to such a challenge is to ensure that while providing low markups, still ensure that there would be no unjustified high prices due to loose monetary and financial conditions. For example, real estate with $10K rent per annum would be priced around $990 K under land ownership restricted to 99 Hijri years under a zero interest rate environment. Imposing a time limit alone will assure ownership and inheritance rights. However, $990K for real estate generating $10K is still on the high end and would not lessen the hoarding motivation, let alone support the affordable housing agenda. The system should discourage land hoarding while encouraging land ownership to generate utility: shelter and food but not rent-seeking. Real estate ownership should be attractive only if individuals create value, not when they are only interested in rent-seeking.

Generally, Zakat is thought to be an instrument to grapple with poverty, inequality, and hunger. However, the main influence of Zakat comes from its role in inhibiting asset hoarding, which leads to monopolistic/oligopolistic price formation. From rulers' perspective, low interest rates, or markup in the case of Islamic finance, are much desired to stimulate the economy. This preference would benefit the present generation at the expense of the next generation (Gundogdu, 2019a, 2019b). The governments should not manipulate the markup on financial activities but be determined in a free market without price collusion of financial institutions or those who have excess funds. Even if the markup rates go to zero, which is not desirable as it would discourage savings, Zakat can fix the issue of asset price bubbles. Zakat is imposed on hoarded real estate, noting that the family shelter is exempted from Zakat calculation at 2.5% based on the asset's market value. This alone would deter land hoarding. Even if we take Zakat to be a 2.5% markup, which is not the case, real estate price will go from $990K to about $365K in a zero interest rate environment. The price would go from $990K to about $27K, $219K, and $180K under a 1, 2, and 3% interest rate environment should the Zakat impose like markup deduction. In reality, however, Zakat should be levied at 2.5% of the asset's market value. In such a case, the house and land prices would go down even further. The imposition of proper Zakat alone would deter real estate investment for speculation and hoarding purposes, and land prices would stabilize in affordability. This policy would encourage people to live in better properties for shelter purposes while deterring hoarding.

Like urban land, agricultural land should not be an object of speculation in low interest rate environments. The 99 Hijra year ownership restriction can be applied as well. On the other hand, agriculture has different parameters for Zakat, as a hadith is presented in Case Box 1.3.

Case Box 1.3: Hadith on Zakat for Agriculture

Jabir b. Abdullah reported the Apostle of Allah (may peace be upon him) as saying: No owner of camels or cattle or a flock of sheep or goats who does not pay his due (would be spared punishment) but would be made to sit on the Day of Resurrection on soft sandy ground. The hoofed animals would trample him with their hoofs and gore him with their horns. And none of them on that day would be without horns or with broken horns. We said: Messenger of Allah, but what is due on them? He said: Lending of the male (for use) and lending of the bucket (used for drawing water for them) and for mating and milking them near water and providing them as a ride for the sake of Allah. And no property owner who does not pay Zakat (would be spared punishment), but it (his property) would turn into a bald snake and follow its owner wherever he goes. He would run away from it, and it would be said to him: That is your property about which you were stingy. And when he would find no other way out, he would thrust his hand in its mouth, and it would gnaw it like a male camel

Source Sahih Muslim, 2167

The hadith gives a valuable clue about the case of Zakat for the agricultural sector. Whether we refer to farms or animals, Zakat is collected from the products. "A tenth is payable on what is watered by rivers, or rains, and a twentieth on what is watered by camels (Sahih Muslim, 981)." Due to cost, the Zakat on irrigated agricultural entrepreneurship is less than unirrigated. Yet, there is no Zakat obligation if the yield is below a certain level: "There is no Zakat payable (on grain or dates) on less than five camel loads. The Wasq (one camel-load) measures sixty sa' in weight (Abu Dawood, 1559)."

In the case of hoarded money, 2.5% of it is due for Zakat payment:

> Pay a fortieth. A dirham is payable every forty, but you are not liable for payment until you have accumulated two hundred dirhams. Five dirhams are payable when you have two hundred dirhams, and that proportion applies to larger amounts. (Abu Dawood, 1572)[4]

The critical point for Zakat's discussion is defining the hoarding level. The hadith provided in Case Box 1.4 gives a hint about hoarding thresholds.

Case Box 1.4: Defining Hoarding Thresholds

I think the Prophet (ﷺ) said: "Pay a fortieth. A dirham is payable every forty, but you are not liable for payment until you have accumulated two hundred dirhams. Five dirhams are payable when you have two hundred dirhams, and that proportion applies to larger amounts

"Regarding sheep, for every forty sheep up to one hundred and twenty, one sheep is due. But if you possess only thirty-nine, nothing is payable on them." He further narrated the tradition of the sadaqah (Zakat) on sheep like that of az-Zuhri

"Regarding cattle, a yearling bull calf is payable for every thirty, a cow in her third year for forty, and nothing is payable on working animals

Regarding (the Zakat on) camels, he mentioned the rates that az-Zuhri mentioned in his tradition. He said: "For twenty-five camels, five sheep are to be paid. A she-camel in her second year will be given if they exceed

---

[4] Abu Dawood, 1561: A man said to Imran ibn Husayn: AbuNujayd, you narrate to us traditions whose basis we do not find in the Qur'an.

Thereupon, Imran got angry and said to the man: Do you find in the Qur'an that one dirham is due on forty dirhams (as Zakat), and one goat is due on such-and-such number of goats, and one camel will be due on such-and-such number of camels?

He replied: No.

He said: From whom did you take it? You took it from us, from the Messenger of Allah (ﷺ).

He mentioned many similar things.

> by one. If there is no she-camel in her second year, a male camel will be given up to thirty-five in its third year. If they exceed by one, a she-camel in her third year will be given up to forty-five. If they exceed by one, a she-camel in her fourth year, ready to be covered by a bull-camel, is to be given." He then transmitted the rest of the tradition like that of az-Zuhri
>
> He continued: If they exceed by one, i.e., ninety-one to hundred and twenty, two she-camels in their fourth year, which are ready to be covered by a bull-camel, are to be given. A she-camel will be given for every fifty in her fourth year if there are more camels. Those in one flock should not be separated, and those who are separated should not be brought together. An old sheep, one with a defect in the eye, or a billy goat is not to be accepted as a sadaqah unless the collector is willing
>
> As regards agricultural produce, a tenth is payable on that which is watered by rivers or rain, and a twentieth on that which draught camels water."
>
> The version of Asim and al-Harith says: "Sadaqah (zakat) is payable every year." Zuhayr said: I think he said, "Once a year."
>
> The version of Asim has the words: "If a she-camel in its second year is not available among the camels, nor is there a bull-camel in its third year, ten dirhams or two goats are to be given."
>
> *Source* Abu Dawood, 1572

In essence, until the hoarding threshold, Zakat can be calculated based on a percentage of income generated from the asset. However, Zakat should be collected based on market value after the threshold. Then, 2,5 percent of money or sheep is due. In the modern world, each country should define hoarding thresholds. For instance, if the threshold for the residential house is 200 m^2, a person can have 100 m^2 for his inhabitance and rent out the remaining 100 m^2. In this case, Zakat on the rent can be calculated akin to irrigated land, that is, 5 percent of the income. The same logic may apply to commercial real estate and agricultural land. After 200 m^2, Zakat should be collected from hoarded assets based on 2.5% of the market value.

Islam's land use policy is different for agriculture to ensure sustainable agricultural production. However, this does not mean hoarding agricultural land without a production motive is permissible. In this case, the key is in the word "hoarding": any land not used for production should be subject to Zakat based on 2.5% of the market value. The land should be available for those who want to produce rather than those intent on rent-seeking. This should not be done by targeting people's ownership rights but by levying Zakat to impede rent-seeking and encourage genuine effort. That is, real estate ownership should be attractive until a certain level. Once it gets to the hoarding level, it must be made unattractive to fulfill the guidance of "Ayah 2:204–205." It is very clear that Islam proposes subtle wisdom, unlike the totalistic approaches of communism and capitalism. Although it might sound appealing, both are extreme, and "they strive throughout the land to spread mischief in it and destroy crops and cattle" (Table 1.3).

The logic of Zakat also would have a reflection on industrial land. Can we collect Zakat based on the market value of a factory? Not really, as factory land, akin to agricultural land, is a factor of production. Similarly, the house used for family shelter is also not subject to Zakat. On the other hand, the provision of collecting Zakat based on yield is only for individuals until the hoarding threshold. For companies, Zakat should be collected based on the Net Worth calculation of shareholders but not as a percentage of the company income.

Hoarding and Ultimate Beneficiary Owner (UBO): Each country should determine the hoarding threshold, such as 200 m^2 for shelter and 10 hectares for farming, based on their country's realities. For instance, agricultural land hoarding levels should be determined to assure commercial viability for scale while encouraging smallholder farmers. Having smallholder farmers across the globe is an effective way of ensuring food security compared to mass-scale landowners making smallholder farming

Table 1.3 Discouraging hoarding of land

	Residential land	Commercial land	Agricultural land	Industrial land
Personal use	No Zakat based on market value	No Zakat based on market value	No Zakat based on market value	No Zakat based on market value
Rent seeking under hoarding threshold	Zakat, based on income	Zakat, based on income	Zakat, based on outputs	Zakat, based on income
Hoarding/speculation	Zakat, based on market value	Zakat, based on market value	Zakat, based on market value	Zakat, based on market value
Time limit for qwnership	99 Hijra years	99 Hijra years	99 Hijra years	99 Hijra years

Source The author

economically unviable due to their scale. Zakat should not be calculated for each property but for the net worth of UBO. Flexibility should be exercised in terms of commercial and industrial land so long as the land is used for economic and productive activities. The Zakat should be calculated based on cash generated from properties so long as holdings are below the hoarding level calculated based on an individual level as indicated in this instruction "Those which are in separate flocks are not to be brought together, and those which are in one flock are not to be separated." This refers to UBO approach to Zakat charging. The phrase "those which are in one flock are not to be separated" means if two partners possessed one hundred and one goats each, three goats were to be given by each of them. When the collector came, they separated their goats. Thus, only one goat was to be given by each of them. This is what I heard on this subject (Abu Dawood, 1571)."

In the case example of a person who has a 200 m^2 house, 10 hectares of agricultural land to produce agricultural commodities, 2,000 m^2 processing factory, and 400 m^2 shop to sell their processed commodities; the Zakat should be calculated based on income but not market value. After hoarding trashold as Zakat should be calculated based on hoarded cash. That is, the national hoarding level for cash should also be defined. If this individual purchases an additional 200 m^2 of housing and 10 hectares of agricultural land, Zakat should be calculated based on the market value of all the assets owned. Not only the real estate hoarded but also the personally used ones should be subject to Zakat based on market value.[5] If a hoarding level is 200 m^2 for a residential unit, a person can use 100 m^2 and rent out the remaining 100 m^2. In this case, Zakat on rent out can be calculated akin to irrigated land, that is, 5%. If the person acquired an additional residential unit of 200 m^2, Zakat should be calculated based on 2.5% of market value from all the assets owned. The same logic would hold for residential land.

"A tenth is payable on what is watered by rivers, or rains, and a twentieth on what is watered by camels (Sahih Muslim, 981)." This hadith is the base of Fatwa's Zakat collection from the income generated from real estate. These Fatwas give people some saving and passive income opportunities as long as they do not cross the hoarding level. After the hoarding

---

[5] The one who has 39 sheeps pays Zakat based on produce, if exceeds 40 sheeps, he pays 2.5% of the assets. Once the hoarding level is exceeded, all the assets are subject to market value Zakat charge.

level is crossed, Zakat should be implemented based on 2.5% of market value on all the assets including personal use ones to inhibit hoarding culture. In this regard, the focus should be on UBO rather than property or the company, as innovative structures are already used for tax evasion and wealth hiding.

Getting a Loan to hoard real estate: Leveraging is extensively used to hoard real estate, and there is an additional motivation in the case of Islamic Zakat obligation. Since leveraging yields negative net worth, there would be motivation to leverage and avoid Zakat. Leveraging to hoard real estate should not be allowed. Conventional finance cannot impose this since any loan can be used for real estate speculation. On the other hand, asset-based and asset-backed embedded features of Islamic finance link the funds with the asset financed directly; hence, such policy is implementable with Islamic finance. Financing real estate until the hoarding level is recommendable in Islam while financing real estate after hoarding should be forbidden.

Another aspect of Zakat in affordable housing is the use of Zakat funds collected. The Islamic proposition is straightforward: collected Zakat should be directly distributed to eligible people. Such people are those facing shelter and food security problems. The Islamic proposition for poverty is not Zakat. Instead, it is a transition tool. The issue should be addressed by encouraging work effort. Creating masses dependent on rich people or the government is not an acceptable notion in Islam (Gundogdu, 2019a, 2019b). Zakat funds cannot be used to produce affordable housing for poor people or develop social infrastructures such as schools, hospitals, water, and sanitation. Social infrastructure development is an unalienable part of affordable housing. The Waqf business model is proposed for social infrastructure (Gundogdu, 2019b). The issue is discussed in greater detail in Chapter 6.

ZAKAT FROM COMPANY SHAREHOLDING

The issue of housing and Zakat for companies is expected to get more attention due to the prevalence of trust or Waqf. It will also attract scrutiny because many real estate hoarders use intermediate companies for tax evasion and would do so for Zakat evasion. Although tax evasion is not Haram in Islam, Zakat evasion is major Haram that could result in severe divine punishment (Gundogdu, 2019a, 2019b).

Case Box 1.5: Mr. Smith
Mr. Smith drew national attention last year when he gave the commencement address at Morehouse College and announced that he would pay off the student loans of the roughly 400 graduates

Federal prosecutors said Mr. Smith had signed an agreement acknowledging his involvement in a 15-year scheme to hide more than $200 million in income and evade millions in taxes by using an offshore trust structure and offshore bank accounts

Under the agreement, the Department of Justice said it would not prosecute Mr. Smith if he paid more than $139 million in taxes and penalties, abandoned $182 million in charitable deduction claims, and cooperated with ongoing investigations

Morehouse College confirmed on Friday that Mr. Smith had made good on his pledge last year when he donated $34 million to pay off the student loans of the graduates of the class of 2019 and the student loan debt of their parents and guardians

Mark E. Matthews, a lawyer for Mr. Smith, declined to comment on Thursday

Mr. Anderson said the agreement showed that "it is never too late to do the right thing."

"Although Smith willfully and knowingly violated the law, Smith has accepted responsibility and agreed to provide complete and truthful cooperation," he said

Federal prosecutors said that Mr. Smith used his unreported income to buy and make improvements to real estate used for his benefit

They said he had used income hidden from taxation to buy and renovate a $2.5 million vacation home in Sonoma, California, to buy two ski properties and a piece of commercial property in France; and to build and make improvements to a home in Colorado that was used charitably for disadvantaged children and wounded veterans

Source *NY Times*

In Case Box 1.5, Mr. Smith agreed to cooperate with tax authorities against Mr. Robert, who hid US$ 2 billion in income in 20 years with whom he cooperated. Evaluating the case from an Islamic perspective shows the following:

- Zakat obligation is calculated not based on any company's income but on individuals' net worth. Zakat cannot be collected from the company or trust. Hence, what matters is the Ultimate Beneficiary Owner (UBO).
- Trust and Waqf have been used for wealth sheltering throughout history (Adiguzel & Kuran, 2021). Hence, the instrumentality of Waqf and its genuine role in social infrastructure development should be well understood.

The subject of company valuation is critical for the Zakat discussion. There are four main groups of widespread company valuation methods: balance sheet, income statement-based, cash flow discounting, and mixed methods, as presented in Table 1.4.

The most accurate valuation method for company valuation is the cash flow discounting method in conventional finance (Fernandez, 2005). It assumes the time value of money and discounts the future cash flow based on the interest rate practiced in the net present value calculation. However, for Zakat purposes, the Zakat is collected from the wealth, that is, net worth (assets minus liabilities). In the case of real estate, after the hoarding level, Zakat is collected based on 2.5% of the market value of all real estate. In the case of companies, the Zakat should not be collected from companies based on the income statement or cash flow. Still, it should be collected from the shareholder based on the market value of

Table 1.4 Company valuation methods

Balance sheet	Income statement	Cash flow discounting	Mixed methods
Book value	Price-earning-ratio	Free cash flow	The classic valuation method
Adjusted book value	Value of the dividends	Equity cash flow	Simplified abbreviated goodwill income
Substantial value	Sales multiples	Capital cash flow	Risk-bearing and risk-free rate method
Liquidation value	Other multiples based on EBIT and ABITDA	Unlevered value plus the discounted value of the tax shield	Annual profit purchase method

Note The list in the table is not exhaustive and suggests commonly used methods
Source Fernandez (2005)

their shareholdings. The market value is available for listed companies based on share prices.

Regarding non-listed companies and SMEs, Zakat's most appropriate valuation method is the adjusted book value. Adjusted book value deducts assets from liabilities after adjusting asset values to reflect the actual market value. However, off-balance sheet contingent liabilities such as guarantees should not be factored in for Zakat purposes. Besides, the land used and machinery for the company's production should not be part of the 2.5% Zakat calculation until the hoarding level. The hoarding level should be defined based on the capacity report of companies that should indicate the land needed for the company. This is similar to the Zakat practice in which a house used for family shelter is not included. Hence, in this delicate balance, there would be no unnecessary stress on the people worrying about their basic assets and hoarding for speculation and rent-seeking. This will allow land to be available for expansion or for companies to be established by future generations or other entrepreneurs. This policy course would lead to an economic structure in which goods and services are provided by numerous SMEs but big corporations. Besides, this would impede stock price inflation, similar to land price inflation, allowing future generations to access assets. To avoid land hoarding in company names, land valuation should adequately be conducted, and Zakat should be reflected in the share values of the shareholders. The Zakat should be collected based on 2.5% of the real estate of Real Estate Investment Trust companies. These companies are vehicles for asset hoarding and are not welcome in an Islamic economic system.

Waqf can also be used to hoard land, money, and real estate to avoid confiscation and Zakat. For Waqf, as long as the land is endowed and used for community, Zakat exemption should be there. However, land ownership should also be limited to 99 Hijri years. It is because Waqf is for the community, which changes over the generation. We should allow the next generations to establish their Waqf based on their priorities.

The Role of Waqf

Similar to Zakat, Waqf has an indirect support function in poverty alleviation. Waqf is not a long-term solution proposed for poverty alleviation in Islam but is a business model for social infrastructure development. Traditional Waqf presents a business model that substitutes private or public ownership. This model is most effective with asset management related to social infrastructure. Examples of such infrastructure include water and sanitation, education, and health. The role played by Waqf should be defined given the improper employment of Zakat funds for economic and social infrastructure like highways, bridges, libraries, schools, and hospitals (Anwar, 1995; Qaradhawi, 1995). Based on the Third Symposium of Zakat Contemporary Issues' Decress No.1 on Zakat Funds investment, permits for the use of Zakat in funding the development of social infrastructure. However, analysis of the prevailing situation would show a contradiction between practice and what is expected regarding wealth distribution. Waqf is supposed to deal with the issue of the development of social infrastructure, which is supposed to be an act of benevolence. On this basis, the Waqf idea developed as a distinct charity implemented in Islam, apart from Zakat. Undoubtedly, as a legal vehicle, the Islamic Waqf model is perceived as an inspiration for secular foundations, endowments, and trusts (Cizakca, 2000). Nonetheless, major differences exist between Waqf and trusts.[6]

Both private and public social infrastructure ownerships have consequences leading to issues related to fairness and sustainability. With its fundamental principles of irrevocability, inalienability, and perpetuity, Waqf ensures that assets are managed in an appropriate manner based on engaging the community to meet basic social infrastructure needs. Regarding private ownership, when human needs are turned into commodities, the inevitable result for society is inequality. In public ownership, the two main issues are related to maintenance and corruption. Waqf presents a feasible business model for engaging communities that benefit from the services of assets (Mawquf Alaihi). However, the application of Waqf throughout history has not been completely connected to the development of social infrastructure. It is common to see people resorting to the Waqf mechanism if they want to avoid paying taxes or having their investments confiscated by the state (Kuran, 2001).[7] Using Waqf in such circumstances is rational behavior. The first reason to support this view is that Islamic economies wave aside tax collection-based

---

[6] For example, in a trust, the property ownership vest with trustee, in case of Waqf ownership vest with Allah. Waqif (Waqf endower) does not have power to revoke Waqf, while in case of trust settlor can revoke trust.

[7] Kuran (2001) provided detailed numbers in case of Ottoman Awqaf in this context.

systems.[8] The second is that Islamic jurisprudence protects inheritance rights to the degree that it is not possible for an individual to allocate all their inheritable assets to Waqf.[9] From this perspective, regarding taxes and limitations to rightful inheritance by the state, individuals often resort to the second most optimal solution: the creation of a family Waqf. The first best option is to have an economic system without tax obligations, and wealth transfer to future generations with inheritance has not been observed. Since Zakat is not collected from Waqf, Waqf can become a real estate hoarding tool.

In Islam, wealth accumulation is encouraged until the hoarding threshold because it leads to people that live independently and have the opportunity to make their voices heard in society. With wealth accumulation until the threshold, people have the kind of resources that will make them voice their concerns in a way that the poor would not when faced with heavy-handedness from the authorities. Therefore, it can be said that when wealth is in the hands of individuals, repression is unlikely to be widespread. However, if wealth accumulation is uncontrolled and only a few individuals or states, like the communist establishments, hold the majority of resources, the benefits of such wealth in averting repression will not be felt by the greater society. For example, when wealth accumulation in the hands of a few leads to the hoarding of real estate, a bigger problem is created since it will undermine shelter provision to families and facility space for companies (Buckley et al., 2009).

The ideal situation is where every person has some assets, and where wealth is not held at the expense of Waqf, Sadaqah, and Infaq. To accomplish this idea, Zakat should be employed as a way of redistributing wealth so that a growing number of people with a certain level of wealth can have a free say on issues affecting the community.

It is vital to discern the connection between Waqf and Zakat. For instance, it must be clear that wealth allocated to Waqf does not constitute a part of the Zakat base. This is the other reason behind the popularity of the family Waqf. Even though tax evasion and protection of assets from

---

[8] Refers to prohibition of tax collection by Muhammad (PBUH) at the establishment of Medina Market. M. J. Kister (1965), "The Market of the Prophet", *Journal of the Economic and Social History of the Orient*, 8(3), 272–276.

[9] Page-33, Obaidullah M. (2013). Awqaf Development and Management. Islamic Research and Training Institute, Islamic Development Bank: Jeddah: Saudi Arabia.

being confiscated may seem like rational causes for family Waqf, it is not acceptable for an individual to avoid Zakat.

The "charity begins at home" principle is associated with Infaq and inheritance, not Waqf. In Islam, the concept of Infaq and inheritance is to prepare kids for the future. Such preparation involves ensuring that they get the highest quality education to prepare them for the changing technology. From a certain degree of inherited wealth, these future generations will generate adequate wealth to sustain their families and contribute to society with Zakat, Waqf, and Sadaqah. Although it is unacceptable to evade Zakat with Family Waqf, as it was presented with cash-in-kind Zakat payment using company shares (Corporate Waqf), paying Zakat can be postponed with a temporary cash Waqf model. However, temporary Waqf does not always meet all the requirements of traditional Waqf: irrevocability, inalienability, and perpetuity. It is equally important to note that these principles are not founded on the teachings of the Qur'an and could be revisited as long as the main aim is to use Waqf to deliver social infrastructure to those that need it. It is possible that the principles of irrevocability, inalienability, and perpetuity of traditional Waqf could have been introduced due to concerns surrounding people who established family Waqf with ulterior motives.

The principles of irrevocability, inalienability, and perpetuity stipulate that a Waqf asset (Mawquf) should not be sold. However, Hukr contracts circumvent this principle, which also permits one to inherit Hukr in practice. Added to this, there are many instances of Istibdal, which involves changing Waqf assets with new assets, and Ibdal, involving changing Waqf assets with cash, recorded in history (Heyneman, 2004). Such practices are already not in keeping with the traditional Waqf principles of irrevocability, inalienability, and perpetuity. Undoubtedly, temporary cash Waqf is tolerable because it is justified with comparable economic benefits for the development of social infrastructure and guarantees Muzakki with financial sustainability concerns. Concerning this, temporary cash Waqf is comparable to the corporate Waqf approach.

While the company's focus is on making as much profit as possible and that of cash Waqf if maximizing return on investment, the dividend payments from a company maximizing profit and the return on investment from cash Waqf can be used in projects involving the development of social infrastructure.[10] Thus, it can be posited that there is a need for a mechanism for developing social infrastructure with cash Waqf and corporate Waqf.[11]

The shareholders in a company or individuals may agree to defer a part of their Zakat obligation with temporary cash Waqf and corporate cash Waqf. This type of postponement is generally acceptable because it deals with apprehensions related to the Muzakki (the party with the obligation to give Zakat) and the Mustahiq (the party eligible to receive Zakat). While the Muzakki may have wealth at a certain period, they may not be sure of the future at a specific moment because economic conditions could change and leave such an individual poor. Thus, when the temporary Waqf is terminated, the concerned individual may have access to wealth. If the conditions improve or remain as they are, that person may continue allocating the wealth to temporary Waqf. Regarding people in need, the return on money in temporary cash Waqf could be invested as Qard Hasan, where the return on investment is used to pay for the development of social infrastructures like water and sanitation, health clinics, and schools. In contrast, the principal amount is returned to whoever originally owned it (Gundogdu, 2018). These social infrastructures are an inalienable part of sustainable cities and the provision of affordable housing. Using temporary Waqf return on investment is an appropriate solution for dealing with needs relating to infrastructure development (Gundogdu, 2018).[12] Obaidullah (2013) provides another definition of Waqf: "withholding an asset while releasing its usufruct."

It can be posited that finite Waqf as a replacement for permanent Waqf could be the solution. From a traditional perspective, Waqf is a business model for delivering social goods, which is better off when not commoditized. Examples of such social goods include water supply, health services, and education. The corporate Waqf or temporary cash Waqf models can better provide resources to develop these social goods if one considers

---

[10] The Cash Waqf seeking high-risk investment for profit maximization categorized as investment bank by some scholar, while Cash Waqf categorized for Waqf administered based on zero-downside risk with moderate return approach.

[11] Obaidullah (2013) provided permissibility of such Waqf in the context of legal comparison across the countries.

[12] Indeed, the men who practice charity and the women who practice charity and [they who] have loaned Allah a goodly loan—it will be multiplied for them, and they will have a noble reward (57:18).

society's changing needs. The models also address the bottlenecks associated with traditional Waqf. The agent/principal problem is more severe in Waqf if there is no mechanism to hinder misappropriation or mismanagement by Nazir/Mutavalli (Trustee-Manager), especially following the death of the Waqif (Waqf Endower). Hence, social infrastructure, such as schools and clinics, should be under the control of the community Waqf, which the inhabitants of the land control.

State Housing Development Projects

Should the state intervene in housing development projects? As a business, no, but for regulating the market with best practices and stabilizing the house prices as part of Hisbah, yes. There are many benefits of state involvement in housing development programs:

- State housing development programs, in collaboration with private developers, can ensure that housing development is done with social infrastructure attached. It also ensures that resilient infrastructure is developed and needed standard elements embedded in the houses.
- The state can set housing development standards.
- State housing programs with private developers would stabilize house prices as it can indicate the price of houses with essential standards.
- State housing programs with developers can institute benchmarks for Islamic mortgage development and securitization.

State housing development entities, delegating construction business to the private sector, can utilize 99 years rotated lands for affordable, green, and resilient housing projects. The expected return on Islamic mortgages can be securitized via Sukuk Ijara and be an investment opportunity for pension funds and Takaful companies. This policy should also accommodate rules and regulations to hinder significant buildings from ensuring the land can be usable by the next generations.

The housing policy should be developed neither with an unbearable fiscal burden on the public sector nor without creating additional risk for the financial sector. The next chapter elaborates on pertinent Islamic perspectives to provide the best model. While this chapter focused on land use policy reform, the next chapter will focus on different financial products and resource mobilization models to provide affordable housing.

References

Adiguzel, F. S., & Kuran, T. (2021, April 22). *The Islamic Waqf: Instrument of unequal security, worldly and otherworldly* (Economic Research Initiatives at Duke (ERID) Working Paper No. 305). Available at SSRN: https://ssrn.com/abstract=3836060

Ahmad, J. J., Mohd, T. I., Huzaimah, I., & Mohd, S. M. (2021). Hisbah Institution and its role in environmental conservation in Islamic civilization. *Jurnal Islam Dan Masyarakat KoNtemporari, 22*(1), 27–35.

Ahmed, Habib. (2004). *Role of Zakat and Awqaf in poverty alleviation*. Islamic Research and Training Institute, Islamic Development Bank Group.

Al-Qaradawi, Y. (1994). *Fiqh al-Zakat*. Maktabah Wahbah.

Anwar, M. (1995). Financing socio-economic development with Zakat funds. *Journal of Islamic Economics, 4*, 15–32.

Buckley R., Chiquier, L., & Lea, M. (2009). *Housing finance and the economy in housing finance policy in emerging markets* (Eds., L. Chiquier & M. Lea). World Bank.

Chiquier, L. & Lea, M. (2009). *Housing finance policy in emerging markets* (Eds., L. Chiquier & M. Lea).. World Bank.(

Cizakca, M. (2000). *History of philanthropic foundations*. Bogazici University Press.

Diallo, A. T., & Gundogdu, A. S. (2021). *Sustainable development and infrastructure*. Palgrave Studies in Islamic Banking, Finance, and Economics, Palgrave Macmillan, number 978-3-030-67094-8.

Egan, M. (1996). *Housing: Diploma in mortgage lending*. The Chartered Institute of Bankers.

Gordon, M. J., & Eli, S. (1956). Capital equipment analysis: The required rate of profit. *Management Science, 3*(1), 102–110.

Gundogdu, A. S. (2018). An inquiry into Islamic finance from the perspective of sustainable development goals. *European Journal of Sustainable Development, 7*, 381–390.

Gundogdu, A. S. (2019a). *A modern perspective of Islamic economics and finance*. Emerald Publishing.

Gundogdu, A. S. (2019b). Poverty, hunger, and inequality in the context of Zakat and Waqf, *30*(1), 49–64. Darulfunun Ilahiyat. https://doi.org/10.26650/di.2019.30.1.0005

Hafidhuddin, D., & Beik, S. (2010). Zakat development: Indonesia's experience. *Jurnal Ekonomi Islam Al Infaq, 1*, 40–52.

Hashim, M. A. (2010, February 16–17). *The corporate Waqaf: A Malaysian experience in building sustainable business capacity* (Paper delivered at Dubai International Conference on Endowments). Dubai, United Arab Emirates. Available at: (accessed on 13 January 2019).

Hassan, M. K. (2010). *An integrated poverty alleviation model combining Zakat, Awqaf, and micro-finance*. Seventh International Conference: The Tawhidi

Epistemology: Zakat and Waqf Economy, 6–7 January 2010, Bangi, Malaysia. Available at: http://www.ukm.my/hadhari/publication/proceedings-of-seventh-international-conference-the-tawhidi-epistemology-zakat-and-waqf-economy (accessed on 13 January 2019).

Heck, P. (2018). *Taxation in encyclopedia of the Qur'ān*. Georgetown University Press.

Heyneman, S. (2004). *Islam and social policy*. Vanderbilt University Press.

Kahf, M. (1989). Zakat: Unresolved issues in the contemporary Fiqh. *IIUM Journal of Economics and Management*, 2, 1–23.

Kister, M. J. (1995). The market of the prophet. *Journal of the Economic and Social History of the Orient*, 8, 272–276.

Kuran, T. (2001). The provision of public goods under Islamic law: Origins, impact, and limitations of the Waqf system. *Law & Society Review*, 35(2001), 841–898.

Madni, A. (2013). The hoarding in Islamic marketing. *IOSR Journal of Humanities and Social Science (IOSR-JHSS)*, 17 (2), 31–38.

Merril, S. (2009). Primary mortgage market infrastructure. In L. Chiquier & M. Lea (Eds.), *Housing finance policy in emerging markets*. World Bank.

Muhtada, D. (2008). The role of Zakat organization in empowering the peasantry: A case study of the Rumah Zakat Yogyakarta Indonesia. In M. Obaidullah & S. Abdullateef (Eds.), *Islamic finance for micro and medium enterprises*. IRTI, Islamic Development Bank.

Myers, N. (1991). *Population, resources and the environment: The critical challenges*. U.N. Population Fund.

Obaidullah, M. (2013). *Awqaf development and management*. Islamic Research and Training Institute, Islamic Development Bank.

Obaidullah, M. (2016a). Revisiting estimation methods of business Zakat and related tax incentives. *Journal of Islamic Accounting and Business Research*, 7, 349–364.

Obaidullah, M. (2016b). *Zakat management for poverty alleviation*. Islamic Research and Training Institute.

Obaidullah, M., & Abdullateef, S. (2011). *Islamic finance for micro and medium enterprises*. Islamic Research and Training Institute.

Orwell, G. (1945). *Animal farm: A fairy story*. Secker and Warburg.

Qaradhawi, Y. (1995). *Fiqh Al-Zakah* (Trans., M. Kahf). Center for Research in Islamic Economics, King Abdulaziz University.

Salehi, D. (2017). Poverty and income inequality in the Islamic Republic of Iran. *Revue Internationale Des Etudes Du Développement*, 1, 113–136.

Siddiqui, A. R. (2008). *Qur'anic key words*. The Islamic Foundation.

Van Order. R. (2003). *Public policy and secondary mortgage markets: Lessons from U.S. experience*. World Bank Global Housing Finance Conference in March 2003.

Williams, J. B. (1938). *The theory of investment value*. Harvard University Press.

CHAPTER 2

Islamic Mortgages and Securitization

Channeling funds for housing development without leading to systematic banking risk

Many conventional finance books are written to perpetuate a system where some become rich at the expense of others in what can be considered a zero-sum game. The Islamic view of finance is based on ensuring that financing tools are utilized in a way to improve the health of society by protecting families that are cornered by the as-is financial system. A significant characteristic of housing finance is the relatively big size and long-term financing horizon. The higher the housing price relative to household income, the longer the tenor gets. The previous chapter discussed the policy course to decrease housing prices. The decreased prices would substantially reduce the resource mobilization needed by the financial sector and risk in resource mobilization and securitization with the decreased time horizon of financing. This perspective is based on the objective of decreasing household debt to spare more resources for future generations' emotional, mental, and physical development. While this policy may be detrimental to land hoarders, bonus getting bankers, it favors society in general. Without integration of housing financing into the formal financial system, however, self-finance with equity or direct finance between individuals gives rise to cities as they are financed: units with low standards and slum proliferation. The Pareto-optimum solution appears to engage the formal financial sector in housing finance with

© The Author(s), under exclusive license to Springer Nature Switzerland AG 2023
A. S. Gundogdu, *Food Security, Affordable Housing, and Poverty*, Palgrave Studies in Islamic Banking, Finance, and Economics, https://doi.org/10.1007/978-3-031-27689-7_2

policy discourse to ensure that household debt and risk to the financial sector are much lower than today. The formal housing system has two parts: lending to households and resource mobilization/securitization to avail more funds for lending.

The Issue of Resource Mobilization and Securitization

An important determinant of success for affordable housing is to design a topography of the financial ecosystem by which the real estate sector does not give rise to systematic financial crises. However, refinance mortgage debt in capital markets has precipitated massive stress on the system. The primary reason is the maturity mismatch between lending and resource mobilization that leads to a liquidity squeeze. Traditional policy reform focused on providing an enabling environment such as enforcing property rights and an effective registration system, developing a comprehensive credit information system, and easy foreclosure for financial institutions to engage in mortgages. The reforms, however, have not factored agency risk of bonus-seeking bankers and real estate appraisers. These reforms led to moral hazard and adverse selection by financial institutions, leading to a subprime crisis. Yet, governments have generally supported this course due to short- and medium-term gains from housing finance as it significantly impacts urban development and economic growth (Renaud, 1999). As discussed in Chapter 1, housing is very interest-sensitive since interest rates hugely impact demand and production. It can easily lead to a liquidity crunch if confidence is lost in the financial sector. Housing can be defined based on a business cycle: low interest rates and hoarding phase, securitization of mortgages which extends low interest rate environment, real estate bubble, higher interest rate environment, a burst of demand and supply, and spread of the failure to the financial system (Buckley et al., 2009). This perspective leads to an important question: Do the policymakers do more of the same things and expect different results? Housing finance supports house price increases, leading to more robust consumer demand, in the short to medium term, even without refinancing for capital gains. Stronger consumer demand is not only associated with more indirect tax collection for public finance, but urban development also provides an environment for some corrupt politicians to raise money for their agendas. The disasters caused by the mismatch are a problem for future generations.[1] What is a paradise for the current generation that will turn into hell for the next generation. There exist both moral hazards and adverse selection in this business model.

The maturity of deposits in deposit-collecting banks, whether Islamic or conventional, is much shorter than the maturity of housing loans. Providing fixed mortgage rates linked to short-term deposit rates would lead to disaster for banks. This maturity mismatch would give rise to liquidity squeezes occurring periodically. Alternative variable rate mortgages are precarious for borrowers. The option of capital markets seems to be more viable. The reality has been the subject of experts in the old days as a benefit of a more capital market-oriented system or more securitized bonds in the secondary market would yield less interest rate risk for borrowers. Any higher interest rate environment can be better managed in capital markets (Laidler, 1974). Nevertheless, risk mitigated in the capital market can also lead to imprudent if the rules and regulations are not imposed under the pretext of financial liberalization.

Previous research suggests that bank-based funding systems suffered larger output losses than capital market-based funding systems during the housing price bust (Barth et al., 2001). Experiences favor capital market-based resource mobilization/securitization against deposit banks' resources. In the case of a capital market system, the issue of currency mismatch is an issue for emerging markets: the use of FX resources would lead to a balance of payment crisis. Mobilizing FX resources to finance housing purchases in local currency would lead to periodic financial crises. However, the side effect of financing for the real estate market should be addressed with policy discourse, as discussed: time limit for land ownership and Zakat on hoarded lands. Figure 2.1 presents the topography in which household deposits or funds from capital markets are used for resource mobilization and securitization.

This business model benefited landowners and real estate developers, assuming there was no corruption inside the bank and municipality. However, the most problematic area of the real estate business is irregularities. Soto (2000) notes that anyone involved in the process would like to get their commission. It can take six months to 14 years, 77 steps through 31 entities, to register property rights to develop desert land in Egypt (Soto, 2000).

---

[1] Rest assure that they don't exist in your country, but this is the fate of unfortunate people of other unfortunate countries.

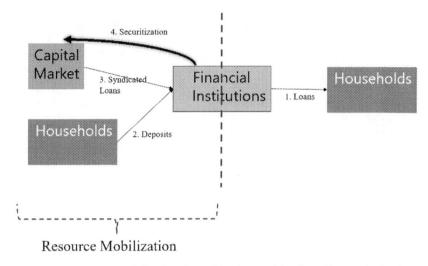

Fig. 2.1 Resource mobilization/securitization and lending (*Source* Author)

Since the assets are not there during the construction phase, there is no securitization possibility to channel funds for construction finance. Financing by buyers and financing of buyers has problems. A developer may end up insolvent and unable to honor their obligations to their suppliers and actual losses due to inflation. Under these circumstances, resources are mobilized from deposit-collecting banks for construction finance. In many countries, the regulators do not prohibit construction finance by the banks. Banks can offer reduced interest rates for a share of the sale price. At first glance, construction lending may appear profitable for the banks, but insight would reveal another aspect, as in the case presented in Case Box 2.1.

Case Box 2.1: Musharaka Real Estate Program of "XYZ" Islamic Bank
In 2014, the CEO and the Vice President in charge of the bank's Marketing decided to prove that "Islamic Finance is for profit-loss sharing." They declared their new initiative in the name of Real Estate Musharaka, by which the bank would enter a partnership with real estate developers: the bank channeled its resources to develop huge residential and commercial properties. In contrast, real estate developers provided

their expertise. The target was to increase the banks' capital by a couple of hundred million dollars in 5 years. From the start of the project, the discounted sales started for early comers. The bank also provided 0.8% per month (the market rate was 1.05% per month) asset-backed Murabaha financing with a ten-year tenor. The bank's CEO and Vice President assured all stakeholders by 2018 that the bank's capital would increase substantially since the real estate investment of the bank would double its value with the accounting practice of revaluation of assets. This will be a significant victory for "profit-loss sharing" Islamic Finance.

Source Author

There are a couple of questions that are worth reflecting on with the case presented:

Question 1: Can a bank legally enter into a partnership for real estate development?

Banks are restricted from holding real assets apart from their direct use, such as HQ buildings or computers. The reason is historical wisdom to ensure that banks are solvent and do not have a liquidity problem. To overcome such regulatory restrictions, special purpose vehicles are used.[2] Special purpose vehicles have legitimate use in Sukuk and public-private partnerships. In the case presented, SPV as a first lien holder has full access to assets and can replace the developer in case of developer failure.

Question 2: Is there any risk management problem with the bank both financing the property development and providing financing to end-buyers?

In this case, the bank finances both the production of the real estate and mortgage phase, increasing the tenor of assets: 2-year real estate development plus two years of a sale campaign plus ten years for mortgage repayment. In this case, the asset-liability and currency mismatch risk exacerbate, and the bank assumes project completion risk and mortgage loan risk together. Any setback during construction or permits from public authorities would put the bank, that is, depositors, in between a

---

[2] A special purpose vehicle (SPV) is a subsidiary legal entity created by a parent company to isolate the financial risk of certain assets, projects, or ventures.

rock and a hard place. As noted, real estate construction is one of the most corrupt businesses globally. Once the banks become part of the practice, this behavioral shift would spread to other practices of banks like cancer. Therefore, the land use policy should discourage land hoarding and corruption. The time limit for ownership and Zakat on hoarded real estate would diminish the drive for hoarding, hence the corruption motivation in the real estate sector.

> *Question 3*: How come the bank could give financing to end-buyers at less than the market rate (0.8% vs. 1.05%)?

Financial institutions take advantage of the general public's lack of financial literacy. They know households would determine their purchase decision based on monthly installments after factoring in their budget and affordability. In this case, the household is encouraged by a lowered interest rate. Real estate developers and banks often get such arrangements, which is more evident in this case as the bank is also a shareholder in real estate development. Recalling from Chapter 1, the real estate price calculation based on the time value of money indicates that the list price of the real estate is higher than the market price. Hence, a lower interest rate is justifiable for the bank. In some cases, real estate developers ask banks for such deals even if the bank is not a shareholder of the development of financier or real estate development, and the real estate developer compensates the bank.

> *Question 4*: The bank's resources comprise an average 3-month local currency deposit and long-term FX loans from the international market. What is the issue with the Assets and Liability risk of the bank?

The bank mobilizes short-term and relatively longer-term FX funds to finance long-term real estate lending. Financing 10-year mortgages with three months deposit certainly gives rise to liquidity strain in due course. The same holds for FX loans, as Islamic banks are not more capable of protecting themselves against currency collapses in the local market they operate. Regarding the maturity and currency mismatch between resources mobilized and long-term mortgage, there will be heavy duty for treasury departments of Islamic banks. This is the leading cause of the heavy use of Shari'ah non-compliant products:

- Bai Al-Inah; sell and lease back.
- Bai Al-Dayn; debt trading, Islamic discounting (factoring).
- Organized Tawarruq; commodity Murabahah.

None of the products above is Shari'ah compliant.

Bai Al-Inah

Rosly and Sanusi (1999) identify *Bai Al-Inah* as one of the most common contract types used when designing Sukuk. In its simplest form, it is a differed sale transaction involving two parties. In the transaction, the individual looking for a loan sells a particular object to the fund's owner. When the cash is advanced, the loan seeker buys the same object with no changes made for a larger amount that will be paid at some date in the future. Many Islamic scholars argue that *Bai Al-Inah* is inappropriate since it is an evasion of a cash loan and, therefore, *Riba*. These scholars are not convinced by the fact that the buyback is not simultaneous following an Ijara. They argue that the most important aspect is the real sale: two sales in a chain among third-party suppliers of the product, loan seeker/debtor, and financier/creditor. In any of the cases, the third-party supplier is missing, which causes concerns. The changed versions of the original *Bai Al-Inah* can be defined as "Sale and Lease back" structures, usually preferred by companies for tax evasion, and made available by conventional leasing companies.

Bai Al-Dayn (Islamic Discounting/Factoring)

> Those who consume interest cannot stand [on the Day of Resurrection] except as one stand who Satan is beating into insanity. They say, "Trade is [just] like interest." But Allah has permitted trade and has forbidden interest. So whoever has received an admonition from his Lord and desists may have what is past, and his affair rests with Allah. But whoever returns to [dealing in interest or usury] – those are the companions of the Fire; they will abide eternally therein. (2:275)

Usually, bill factoring or discounting is suggested as similar to *Murabaha*, and hence alternatives that result in Shari'ah compliance in trade finance. Specific Murabaha features make it a suitable alternative for trade finance and offer the economy protection from the systematic risk inherent in orthodox finance methods for the following reasons:

 i. Relating to Murabaha, the disbursement is done to the supplier of the account, which provides better risk assessment opportunities for banks and ensures that the debtor uses the funds for production instead of speculative or unproductive causes.
 ii. On the disbursement date, the sale price and repayment dates are defined. If any delays occur regarding repayment, it is impossible for the financier to accrue late payment charges to their account. For this reason, the financier must do their due diligence to ensure that they are giving credit to a creditworthy individual.
 iii. Since Murabaha's finances enable genuine transactions, the likelihood of them leading to a credit bubble is small. Even though Islamic finances get closest to discounting or factoring in export financing, there is still a considerable difference: recourse to those seeking loans. Regarding Murabaha-linked Islamic export finance, the financier cannot resort to the loan seeker (exporter) and should wait for the importer to repay, meaning that the bank takes the risk of a final buyer. Relating to factoring/discounting, the financier can provide resources to the loan seeker. With all these features, Islamic finance differs from debt trading in that it does not lose its link to the real economy. For this reason, many posit that it should not result in a credit bubble (Gundogdu, 2016).

Organized Tawarruq: *Commodity* Murabaha

Nowadays, the majority of Islamic banks' Murabaha syndications, interbank lending, and hedging tools, such as Islamic SWAPS, are founded on organized Tawarruq. This is an issue comprehensively discussed by Gundogdu (2014) using the example of a lean seeker (Resource Mobilizing Bank) and a possible lender (Liquidity Managing Bank) in transactions involving precious metal contracts with cash through commodity traders. The Liquidity Managing Bank purchases a metal contract. It makes a deferred sale to the Resource Mobilizing Bank, which sells the contract to another commodity trader that pays in cash. On maturity, the Resource Mobilizing Bank repays the differed sale price to Liquidity Managing Bank.

Initially, there was only one commodity trader, and after extensive criticism by *Shari'ah* critics, a second commodity trader was introduced. Nonetheless, the structure is still organized Tawarruq, which the Islamic Fiqh academy disallowed. The reason was that this was not perceived as a regular Tawarruq but rather an organized act put in place to circumvent cash landing restriction of Islamic Shari'ah. Other banks resorted to common stock instead of precious metal contracts and other more convincing forms. However, from the perspective of *Maqasid Al-Shariah*, it is clear that there are obvious flaws. The entities participating in this transaction are not financing or facilitating bona-fide economic activity but could be said to create debt out of nothing. Figure 2.2 illustrates the commodity Murabaha based on Tawarruq. No link exists between the precious metal contracts and physical metal stock. This is the challenge that Gundogdu (2014) exclusively dwells on. The same scholar suggests an alternative Shari'ah-compliant two-step Murabaha arrangement used in international trade finance for interbank lending.

Another issue with resource mobilization in Islamic finance is that financing contracts are often confused with resource mobilization contracts. While encouraging Islamic finance, resource mobilization contracts are proposed with the pretext of Islamic Finance being a profit-loss sharing business model. Indeed, Islamic finance is profit-loss sharing

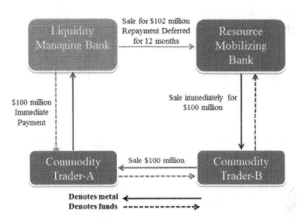

Fig. 2.2 Organized *Tawarruq* with commodity *Murabaha*. (*Source* Gundogdu [2014])

for those who want to lend their excess funds. The funds should be mobilized with resource mobilization contracts and lent forward with financing contracts. It is important to note that resource mobilization has securitization and liquidity management facets. For instance, assets produced with resources mobilized can be securitized and be subject to liquidity management for the financial institution.

Fund providers can put funds together for a profit-loss sharing venture with a Mudaraba to finance agricultural commodity trade with Murabaha or agricultural production with a Salam contract. The fund provider shares the prof-loss of their venture, while the fund seeker is tied with liability to repay. The profit-loss sharing relationship should be among fund providers, not between fund providers and fund seekers who would exploit the situation (Gundogdu, 2019). Similarly, house purchases can be financed with Murabaha or Ijara contracts. Istisna contracts can be used to produce houses; that is, they can be used to finance construction.

Islamic Mortgages and Lending

Housing finance constitutes a substantial proportion of the GDP in all economies. The residential mortgage market amounts to the bulk of the GDP of developed countries, and emerging economies are in the same course. This is why the real estate and banking crises are highly correlated. Buckley and Kalarickal (2006) describe this: "… the housing genie is out of the bottle." Perhaps, two factors lead to this trend: houses deemed as secure collateral against which banks are willing to lend and house hoarding motivation by individuals in a low interest rate environment harnessed with financial liberalization. Similarly, housing finance should not be encouraged for hoarding purposes but for providing shelter for the people.[3] The sub-prime crisis provided real-life insight into the matter.

Hernando de Soto (2000) argues that with low interest rates, low-income borrowers can raise capital by pledging their property as they don't have an alternative to access capital from the formal financial sector. Providing low interest rates may work as long as increased bidding with more mortgages does not increase house prices. Some policies, rules, and regulations are needed to make the financial system work for a good cause. That is, we are not in a fairy tale, and genie should stay in the

---

[3] Banks assume housing financing as secure way of lending with easy collateral taking and unjustified trust for everlasting house price increase.

bottle under control. The borrower should be getting affordable loans over the life of the loan, while the lender should be getting an acceptable risk-adjusted return, and this should be done without precipitating systematic financial sector risk. For instance, fixed-rate mortgages would work at the expense of investors and lead to systematic financial sector risk if deposit banks' resources are used during the inflationary economic environment. The problem will worsen if FX resources finance local currency mortgages. This is how Mexican banks went bankrupt in the early 80s (Lea, 2009). Today, several OIC countries make similar mistakes.

The situation under Shari'ah Law is even direr since there is no way to change the sale price. Additionally, there is no Shari'ah room to mitigate such risks in capital markets with SWAPs. These Shari'ah restrictions would prompt FIs to be more prudent and conceal the issues until they become systematic financial sector failures. Since Islamic finance involves the sale or leasing of a house to the borrower, the price is fixed at the beginning of the loan term. Hence, Adjustable-Rate Mortgages (ARMs) or Indexed Mortgages (IM), being inflation, interest rate, or FX indexed, are not permissible in Shari'ah. ARMs were the leading cause of the subprime crisis in the USA that turned into a systematic financial sector risk. This alone proves the merit of Shari'ah restriction for the overall benefit of society and the superiority of divine guidance over fairy assumptions of too-smart-to-miscalculate humans. Falling house prices debunked the basic assumption, and such a debacle shall repeat until humanity gets wise enough to be humble and ask for divine guidance.

The primary mortgage infrastructure developed, particularly mortgage-related insurance products, can substantially exacerbate systematic risk. Availability of catastrophic, property, and mortgage life insurance guards lenders against collateral risk. The actuarial calculation, however, would not work in a moral hazard and adverse selection environment. Takaful's Islamic business model for insurance is permissible as long as the transaction promotes trade and investment and impermissible if insurance leads to moral hazard and adverse selection (Gundogdu, 2019). For instance, with mortgage default insurance, profit-driven banks and bonus-seeking bankers would extend loans to unqualified borrowers. Besides, they would prefer unqualified borrowers to overqualified ones as they can charge more by assuming that the underlying security package and higher interest rate compensate for the so-called delicately calculated higher default risk.

In addition to mortgages, several methods of housing finance, such as microfinance, developers' finance, rental finance, and loans without a pledge, are beyond the scope of this book. The Islamic Banks use *Murabaha, Ijara, and Diminishing Musharaka* and Istisna contracts for house financing. As noted, using Musharaka, a resource mobilization tool, is improper for home financing. In practice, diminishing Musharaka is often used for house financing, though. Istisna is an asset development contract that can be used to finance real estate development. There is a specific benefit of banks' involvement with Istisna contracts:

i. Bank can manage the purchase contracts and procurement and ensure quality-cost-based best selection.
ii. Allow policy to build resilient buildings against natural disasters such as earthquakes and floods.
iii. May allow direct public for renewable energy, environmentally friendly, and durable materials.

Yet, Istisna contracts cannot be used for financing finished real estate. Although households are financed with not only Musharaka but also both Murabaha and Ijara contracts by Islamic Banks, the proper way is to use Ijara contracts but not Murabaha.

Murabaha as Practiced by Islamic Banks for House Financing

In the literal sense, the term Murabaha denotes a profitable sale. It is also known as Bai' Bithaman Ajil, meaning that it is a sale where payment is deferred. Based on such a definition, Murabaha represents an installment sales contract. Out of all the Islamic approaches regarding leveraged home acquisition, this is the method most in keeping with traditional house purchase processes. Murabaha denotes a kind of asset finance involving the lender buying the asset and then selling it to the borrower at a higher price. The interest that would have been payable is represented by the increased price (Kettell, 2011). A Murabaha financing case is provided in Case Box 2.2.

Case Box 2.2: Islamic Home Financing; Murabaha Case of Davon Bank

As a community bank, the Chicago (USA) bank known as Devon Bank works toward meeting the financial services needs of customers from different walks of life. This implies that it seeks to make services available for financial transactions that have to meet specific religious principles like those stipulated by Islamic religious law (Shari'ah). For example, Islamic law does not allow interest to be paid to a bank following a lending transaction, even though profit payment is permitted. On this basis, Devon Bank works hard to ensure that the needs of such individuals are met when involved in transactions like buying a home. Devon Bank has the policy to provide rates that are competitive when compared to peers. The financial institution illustrates its commitment to its policy by availing of religious finance programs that do not allow interest to be collected. Nonetheless, religious-based transactions cannot run away from costs associated with them that may stand on the verge of failing to meet the requirements of Shari'ah. The additional costs depend on the degree of complexity and documentation needed to meet specific religious concerns.

A Murabaha contract delivers an appropriate contrivance to buy a home without the added complexity while still ensuring that the purchase is structured in a manner that no interest is involved. A typical Murabaha transaction includes a purchase with deferred payment resale. At Devon bank, the customer identifies the house they want the bank to pay for on their behalf. The customer I was responsible for negotiating the house price and other related aspects. It is also their responsibility to make any required payments to ensure that Devon can start the process. Devon then steps into the transaction and buys the property. Immediately, the bank sells the house to the customer for a fixed price—which is calculated by adding the bank's profit to the purchase price. The bank's customer can then pay the aggregate price in an initial down payment and fixed installments over the agreed period.

All the direct costs endured by Devon Bank, like recording costs, taxes, and appraisal fees, are paid by the customer when the deal is closed. Once a commitment has been issued, a deposit is paid and applied to such costs at closing. Once the deal is closed, apart from a couple of added religious recommendations, the relationship going forward is no longer different from that of a conventional mortgage. The customer signs the Murabaha contract with Devon Bank stipulating that the mortgage is free from interest. However, laws in the USA require the bank to calculate the corresponding interest and report that rate to the customer. The bank also

> must send disclosures to the customer indicating any interest paid every year, which could be deductible from Tax.
> *Source* Kettell (2011)

Understanding the defining lines of collateral-taking is necessary as asset-backed and asset-based contracts have different aspects. What makes asset-based Murabaha different from a conventional loan? Indeed, asset-based Murabaha and conventional mortgages are very similar, yet the defining line is late payment charges. Islamic banks cannot and should not incur late payment fees. This would urge banks to be more prudent in their lending practice. Shari'ah restriction, in this way, contributes to the financial stability of the system.

Asset-based contracts are also not suitable for securitization. We should seek contracts connecting the green field with the capital market without leading to systematic risk. Lien on real estate with asset-based Murabaha would suffice for risk management for banks. Besides, since there is no asset ownership, bank-financed mortgages cannot be securitized in Islamic finance. Asset ownership is needed. However, using asset-backed Murabaha would convert Murabaha into an Ijara agreement since the ownership remains with the bank. It can be discerned that from both the lending and securitization aspects, neither asset-based nor asset-backed Murabaha is the best match, but Ijara is.

Ijara as Practiced by Islamic Banks House Financing

In the case of trade finance, Murabaha is the proper contract that transfers money and ownership for fast-moving products. This is not the case with house financing, by which there is no reason to expect a level of real property expertise from households that would, probably, have one purchase in a lifetime. Given the obligation of asset maintenance and continued bank obligation on the asset, Ijara, not Murabaha, is the suitable Islamic contract for financing shelter needs of houses; a case is presented in Case Box 2.3.

Case Box 2.3: Islamic Home Financing; Ijara Case of Manzil Home Purchase of Ahli United Bank

This is a lease-to-own scheme. Under the Manzil Ijara scheme, the property is registered in the bank's name initially and throughout the lease. The process is as follows:

(i) The customer indicated the property they wanted to purchase and negotiated the purchase price with the seller.
(ii) The customer applies to Manzil for financial assistance for purchasing the property.
(iii) Manzil purchases the property in its name after it is satisfied that everything is in order.
(iv) Using an agreement called "Promise to Purchase," Manzil sells the property to the customer. The customer buys the property at the same price as the original purchase price.
(v) As soon as the property has been purchased, the customer and Manzil enter into a lease detailing the customer's rights to occupy the property.
(vi) Based on the lease agreement, the customers make monthly payments to Manzil.
(vii) Every monthly payment is calculated in such a way that part of it is used to pay for the purchase of the property and part of it for rent.
(viii) The monthly installment is fixed every 12 months between April of a specific year and April of the next. At the beginning of April each year, Manzil assesses the rent payments.
(ix) At any time during the contract, the customer reserves the right to purchase the property from Manzil.

The Manzil Ijara arrangement stipulates that the property is registered in the name of the bank, not just in the beginning but throughout the tenure of the agreement. The relationship is based on the agreement between the bank and the customer that the latter will eventually buy the property at the same price paid by the bank without any markup. The payments by the client every month consist of three elements:

- The rent paid for the property constitutes the bank's profit. The bank reassesses the rent every year to ensure that it is making a reasonable return and is adjusted downward based on what the customer has already paid.

> - An insurance premium aimed at covering the costs borne by the bank to insure the property.
>
> The monthly payments can increase or reduce over time. Whichever direction they move depends on the size of the first repayment element that the customer decides they can afford. When the customer pays the bank too early, the bank does not make much profit unless the bank has a way of getting a higher return after reinvesting the funds.
>
> *Source* Kettell (2011)

If they do not have a stake in an Ijara agreement, banks and real estate developers will shun their obligations in case of a problem with the house developed. However, the content of the Ijara agreement should be Shari'ah compliant, hence keeping banks' obligations without transferring risks to customers with circumventive clauses. Banks would be more prone to short-term gains rather than long-term sustainable houses without paying attention to this. Forcing banks to have a stake in a house with Ijara would develop sustainability criteria in engaging housing projects. Banks would seek houses that will not be defective in 10 years. Also, they would look for environmental resilience. For instance, they would not finance houses in flood or earthquake zones. Enforcing the Ijara contract would lead banks and constructors to deliver high-quality and resilient houses, ensuring added value as households cannot discern defects at first glance. The critical thinking and the fact that Islam has different financing contracts for different transactions suggest that Ijara contracts should be used to finance household home purchase and construction should be financed by Istisna contracts. How about mobilizing resources to channel funds to households: it requires deliberation on Islamic reflection on resource mobilization and securitization in financial markets.

Islamic Resource Mobilization

Resource mobilization for construction and house purchase finance is required before securitization in the secondary market. Construction finance involves land development and building construction. Low-standard houses and slums may emerge without a well-functioning construction finance system. Sustainable Development Goals (SDGs) for sustainable cities necessitate the provision of housing with specific standards and social infrastructure.

Mobilizing resources for construction has different features than house purchase mechanisms. Most importantly, there is a performance risk as the developer may not finish the construction. Performance bonds and insurance policies were introduced to guarantee the completion of construction projects in developed countries to mitigate the risk. The issue of moral hazard and adverse selection emerged as banks selected more profitable developers than efficient and reliable developers; instead, they rely on performance bonds. In some developing countries, alternative mutual guarantee funds sponsored by the government are instituted to protect pre-sale home buyers against non-completion risk (Chiquier, 2009).[4]

There are different types of Islamic home purchase cases. Purchasing parts are similar and can be done with the Islamic finance contract. The difference comes from the way resources are mobilized. The lack of house and construction financing resources led to creative schemes across Organization of Islamic Cooperation (OIC) countries. The main issue with these schemes is that they collect deposits like commercial banks without the government's supervision and regulation. Even with the banks under regular and vigorous supervision and regulation, depositors can lose their hard-earned money. The case is riskier with innovative schemes. The cases of crowdfunding for construction finance and Islamic Rent-Supporter Lottery for house financing will be discussed for more insight.

Ethis Crowdfunding, Indonesia[5]

The crowd financing model is already perceived as an alternative method to deposit banking for construction finance. In fact, it will enable the creation of an independent financial architecture due to the opportunities for investors and entrepreneurs to provide direct transaction avenues. Unlike the fund pools that deposit banking contains, it will also be stripped of Gharar.

---

[4] Getting operational in 2000, the fonds de Garantie & de Caution Mutuelle de la promotion Immobiliere of Algeria is one of the examples for such funds.

[5] Based on MA thesis of Ayhan Yuksel under the supervision of the author. "Analysis of alternative capital sources for the financing of ventures: An approach within the framework of Islamic economics," 2021.

The Indonesia-based Ethis crowdfunding platform is an initiative based on the principle of halal investment. Ethis provides funding not only for business ideas but also for many projects, from infrastructure projects to social housing projects, from machinery supply to home financing. Ethis crowdfunding describes itself as the "First Shari'ah-compliant property crowdfunding platform." The platform has mediated the construction of more than 9,200 houses, the realization of more than 1400 investments, and the creation of 133.4 million dollars in value. Generally, a dividend of 9–13% per annum is distributed from the investments made. The investments' maturities have an average of 9–24 months.

Examples of project financing using Islamic financial instruments are provided below.

Case: Hyang Salinas Village
Project Terms:

> Return for crowdfunding investors: 14% for retail investors and 15% for institutional investors
> Project Duration: 12–13 Ay
> The total investment required: SGD 119.323,00
> Project description: 26 Affordable houses within 12 months
> Project partner for construction: PT Cipta Darma Abundan (PT CDA)
> Project collateral: PPJB—Conditional sale and purchase certificate of the four housing units. A post-dated cheque higher than the total value of the crowd-funded amount. Personal guarantee from the director of PT CDA

The project is defined in two phases: construction and sales of finished houses. The construction phase is administrated with an Istisna contract. On the other hand, the finished houses are sold with Murabaha. Figure 2.3 presents Phase 1.

Phase 2 is provided in Fig. 2.4.

The units are planned to be sold at a minimum of IDR 527 Mil (approximately SGD 51,000). The Indonesian government has a "1 million Home" program, which has no cap on the price of affordable housing units. The housing units are classified as commercial and residential housing in this project. Ethis identified the main risk as unforeseen

ISTISNA' AGREEMENT

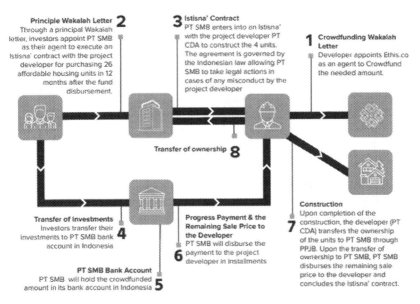

Fig. 2.3 Phase 1, Istisna contract for construction (*Source* Ethis crowdfunding)

delays in the sales of the units to the end-buyers. The main risk is identified for investors to ensure the return of their capital plus a markup.

Ethis call for investors to join resource mobilization with the following features:

(i) Asset-backed: there is a fallback on tangible assets.
(ii) Profitable: 14% return for a minimum investment of SDG 1,000 (called Retail Investors) and 15% return for a minimum investment of SDG 20,000 (called Silver Investors).
(iii) Social Impact: homes are intended to be provided to low-income families.

Resource mobilization with crowdfunding is commendable. Heavy exposure of deposit-collecting bank resources to real estate gives rise to systematic risk. The issue, however, is allowing fund collection that may

46   A. S. GUNDOGDU

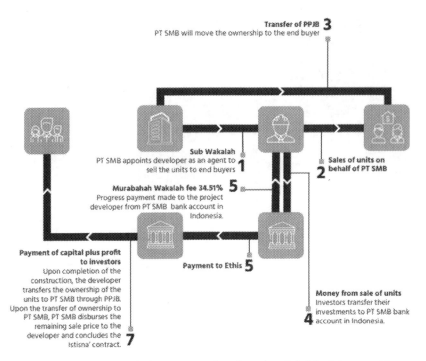

Fig. 2.4 Phase 2, Murabaha contract for the sale of finished houses (*Source* Ethis Crowdfund)

lead to embezzlement of funds and victimization of investors. Commercial banks collect a deposit, yet they are under the tight control of central banks and banking regulatory and supervisory authorities. Similar institutional infrastructure is needed to enable crowdfunding to blossom: one bad example can destroy the reputation of the crowdfunding business. Developing the assets with the Istisna contract is a proper implementation of Islamic finance. However, using Murabaha to sell finished houses mitigates risk for the constructor and crowdfunding investors. The motivation is to finish quickly and cost-effectively so that sustainability of houses could be ignored. Adding some features to houses against natural hazards such as floods and earthquakes to enhance resilience benefits households and the government as the damage would be manageable in case of natural hazards. Adding resilience features, however, would decrease the profit margin of investors and motivate them to avoid extra costs. In the end, having resilient houses is in countries' best interest, and government should note such motivation. For instance, the use of Ijara, in which investors keep a steak in the asset, instead of Murabaha, in which investors transfer assets without any steak to the household, would urge investors to think about the long-term sustainability of the asset.

Islamic Rent-Supporter Lottery System, Turkey

Islamic rent-supporter lottery systems have been introduced as a novelty across OIC countries. Indeed, they are akin to early building societies that emerged in Anglo-Saxon countries, where savings of lower- and middle-income households were collected for home construction. The members pledged to have a regular contribution to society by building houses, and houses were allocated by lottery. The lottery would continue until each member was housed if the society persisted. The system strayed once the system accepted the purchase of a finished house with professional managers. The system would later transform into the Building Societies/Savings and Loan (S&L) model. The S&L model lost ground to commercial banks with financial liberalization in the 80s. That liberalization allowed commercial banks to enter the sector. The collapse of the S&L model would also be attributed to the inability to manage risk associated with short-term variable rate liability vs. fixed-rate loans (Mason, 2004). The more than a century journey from building and loans to bail out showed that the issue of asset and liability mismatch is the hinging point in housing finance.

The section dealing with the issues of resource mobilization discusses the use of Arabic names, such as Bai Al-Inah and Bia Al-Dayn, to package Shari'ah non-compliant schemes. Similarly, there is a trend of laundering Shari'ah non-compliant schemes using Islamic terminology. Lottery is forbidden in Islam, yet many lottery-based so-called Islamic house solidarity establishments flourished. They claim they support devout Muslims to have houses without mingling with Riba bank loans. The scheme is shown in Fig. 2.5.

Participants should be as many as the number of installments required, making it possible to make one participant a monthly homeowner based on the installments collected. The participants decide the size of the house they want to buy and the number of installments they want to pay, with the organizer taking care of the rest. At a casual glance, this may look simple, but in reality, it is not. The number of installments is determined

Fig. 2.5 Rent-supporter lottery system (*Source* EminEvim)

by the people participating. The installments decrease until the participant gets a house. After the participant gets a house, the installment will increase before it gets fixed until they complete their installments. The lucky ones get their houses early. A sharp house price decrease can lead to the system tumbling. This is in addition to the difficulty of being a non-bank in managing asset and liability mismatches as they don't have a central bank as a lender of the last resort in case of emergencies.

Crowdfunding has problems related to fund-collecting. The lottery system, in addition to the problem related to funding collection, has Shari'ah compliance problems. It leads to people escaping from Riba but ending up entangled in Maysir and Gharar. Affordable housing can be achieved by policy shift: not using deposit-collecting banks' resources but using crowdfunding for the construction phase and tradable Sukuk Ijara for securitization. This Sukuk can be a good investment instrument for pension funds and Takaful companies. Not only S&Ls but also specialist mortgage banks lost their share to commercial banks with the deregulation that empowered commercial banks in the 80s. However, they have developed a successful securitization system and asset and liability management. The issue with mortgage banks was a limited reach as compared to commercial banks that purchase many mortgage banks (Lea, 2009). We need to note lessons learned for the next level.

The Next Level Housing Program

The history of the housing finance system reveals two successful business models that, in turn, lost ground to commercial banks in the 80s due to risk management issues (for S&Ls) and limited market reach (for mortgage banks). Initial building societies that mobilized resources from the crowd did not have major risks until they transformed into S&Ls. Mortgage banks developed a sound securitization system. This fact provides valuable lessons for a robust and easy-to-access Islamic housing finance architecture: the Shari'ah problem of a lottery with building society is not there with Ethis crowdfunding, and mortgage banks' securitization can be transformed into Islamic Sukuk. Note that the more conventional finance deals with the actual transaction, the more it resembles Islamic finance, which is the case with mortgage banks and building societies, yet assuring that the elements of *Gharar*, *Maysir*, and *Riba* are not part of the financial agreements.

Based on the discussion so far, the parameters are defined as:

- Do not resort to deposit-collecting commercial banks for real estate development. Crowdfunding is a viable alternative to impede systematic banking risk. However, the fund collection of crowdfunding companies should be heavily regulated, akin to commercial banks, to assure sound risk management and inhibit fraud.
- Use the Istisna contract to assure that crowd investors have some stake in assets developed to ensure long-term sustainability.
- Securitize the deal with Ijara Sukuk to mobilize resources from capital markets after Ijara contracts with home buyers. The return on Sukuk should be lower than the return of crowd investors as they take more risk. Crowd investors can be individuals, while Sukuk investment is more suitable for risk-averse long-term institutional investors such as pension funds and Takaful companies.

Ideal Islamic housing development strategy should harness lending with proper resource mobilization. The lending, resource mobilization, and financing aspect should also support the sustainability of the housing developed. In this regard, there is a need to unbundle the Islamic mortgage value chain to delegate risk and return based on the capacity and appetite of actors in the value chain, as presented in Table 2.1.

Table 2.1 Matching lending and resource mobilization

	Lending	Resource mobilization/securitization
Real estate development	Istisna	Crowdfunding
Purchase by household	Ijara	Sukuk

Source Author

For construction, resources should be mobilized, and it can be done from crowd-funders with local currency, guaranteeing that there would be no maturity mismatch. Since tenors are longer with mortgages, the best way is to securitize the mortgages with Sukuk and make them available to Islamic FIs, including Takaful Companies and Pension Funds, for hold-to-maturity, after the crowd-funders deliver assets. This would bring about a liquidity management platform for Islamic banks as a remedy to the liquidity management problem of Islamic Banks. While doing such securitization, it should be ensured that risk obligations are earmarked properly. For instance, any risk associated with asset production should be borne by crowd-funders as per the obligation of the Istisna contract. This would urge crowd-funders to work with reputable constructors. The Sukuk should be issued only after the production of assets with defect obligation should be on crowd-funders. Sukuk holders should bear the risk of non-payment of Ijara receipts yet keep ownership of assets. There should be no Gharar in the form of diluting good and bad risk, as was the case with the mortgage-backed securitization example of the 2008 financial crisis. Sukuk holders should have transparent access to information on the risk and valuation they assume for the asset they have lien vis-à-vis expected return. Since crowd-funders assume more risk, such as guaranteeing the sustainability of houses for ten years, their return should be much higher than Sukuk investors. Selecting a securitization agent is key as they link production with securitization. The most challenging part of securitization is late payment charges. Islamic Shari'ah does not allow the imposition of late payment charges as it is deemed, Riba.

Securitization agents should make proper calculations to mitigate this risk. The historical perspective suggests that the involvement of deposit-collecting banks or their subsidiaries in mortgage securitization turned out to be malefic. The Keystone Bank case is presented in Case Box 2.4.

Case Box 2.4: The Glass-Steagall Act
The First National Bank of Keystone in West Virginia started buying and securitizing subprime mortgages across the United States in the early 1990s. This resulted in the bank growing from a small bank with a little over $100 million in assets to one with assets valued at more than $1.1 billion. This led the bank to the top of the list of the most profitable large community banks in the United States. However, it would soon be discovered that all the supposed success was on the back of fraudulent activities.

All the securitization deals the bank was involved in hemorrhaged money. The company executives hid this through sophisticated manipulation of the books. This also helped them hide that they were siphoning millions of dollars from the bank. The bank's managers hid all the fraud from almost everybody, including the bank's board of directors, federal banks examiners, auditors, and attorneys. The examiners were kept at bay by frustrating their efforts to access any documents they were entitled to during duty. These were documents that the bank's executives knew would expose their elaborate and illegal schemes. To show how desperate the company executives were, the bank's head went as far as to bury four truckloads of documents underground in her ranch The Federal Deposit Insurance Corporation billed for the estimated amount of US$780–820 million. The Glass-Steagall Act became law in 1933 and aimed to separate commercial banking activities from investment banking in response to the involvement of commercial banks in the stock market. The Gramm-Leach-Bliley Act eliminated the Glass-Steagall Act's limits against connections between commercial and investment banks in 1999, which could be seen as the event that set up the stage for the 2008 financial crisis.

Source Pasley (2017)

It is not just the deposit-collecting banks that have not met the bill's conditions but also state housing banks (SHBs). State housing banks have been frequently bailed out and rescued with public money in many countries. This has been the case across different geographies. The Indonesian experience is described in Case Box 2.5.

Case Box 2.5: Bank Tabungan Negara, Indonesia
Bank Tabungan Negara was established to distribute subsidized housing loans. The bank was funded by the central bank with privileged conditions and held a monopoly of subsidized loans. It was permitted to extend 20-year loans that the private sector could not provide. Although the bank was charging large intermediation margins and had an 80% market share, it still permed bald. Its delinquency ratio reached 25% by the end of the 80s. The performance put the bank in a precarious financial situation. Its managers took action, and the bank improved financial management. However, at the same time, the bank expanded into corporate lending to diversify its portfolio. However, it did not have the capacity for corporate loans. During the 1997 crisis, 100% of corporate loans defaulted. Bank

> Tabungan Negara transferred its impaired loans to the agency in charge of restructuring the banking system with a bill of $1 billion, more than 20 times the housing subsidy budgeted yearly.
> *Source* Hasler and Renaud (2009)

Policy discourse of deterring real estate hoarding would stabilize housing price fluctuation and make asset-liability management much easier. Unlike the experience with the subprime crisis, Islamic finance principles contain failure based on the project base, as each mortgage is directly linked to the secondary market. In the worst case, Sukuk investors have access to the financed real estate, which requires substantial mortgage enforcement rights. The feature impedes systematic risk and protects Sukuk investors' rights. This system would spotlight capable crowdfund managers, constructors, and securitization agents. Talent in doing business would be the main criterion for success. The strict Shari'ah restrictions would promote a merit-based business environment rather than as-is networking and corruption.

The success of the next-level housing program depends on an enabling environment. Such an environment involves a comprehensive legal framework for Islamic mortgage lending, an adequate legal framework for property ownership, and macroeconomic stability. Although the imposition of Zakat on real estate hoarders would decrease the price, reducing the amount and tenor of mortgages, production cost, and construction time still would necessitate some tenor. This is more critical in the case of Islamic mortgages, as fixed-rate mortgages (FRM) are the only alternative in Islamic finance. Shari'ah prohibits Adjustable-Rate Mortgages (ARMs) or Indexed Mortgages (IM). And there is no room for Shari'ah compliance SAWP or derivative option for secondary market hedging.

Islamic financial institutions (FIs) are more prone to liquidity risk in an unstable macroeconomic environment. Yet, this shortfall decreases the contagion of an FI failure and is good for avoiding systemic risk generated in the derivative market that undermines macroeconomic stability. Systematic risk forces central banks to intervene to reduce interest rates and increase the money supply that feeds into higher house prices (Gundogdu, 2019). Macroeconomic stability is also key for credit risk, measured by the probability of default and loss given default. Macroeconomic stability reduces the possibility of abrupt decreases in house prices and the related economic slowdown that could trigger unemployment. The more the ratio of mortgage payment to monthly income ratio of monthly debt service decreases, the less the credit risk gets. As discussed, the most effective way to ensure this is to decrease house prices by imposing Zakat on hoarders. The market risk associated with such elements as real wages, inflation, exchange rates, and interest rates created by central banks gives rise to bigger economic problems. It could be a harbinger of higher systematic risks in future financial markets. Conventional finance risk mitigation methods and mechanism novelty have yielded no results. The public, primarily the low-income segment, paid bills due to central bank interventions and government bailouts or fallbacks for the risk mitigation novelty.

The discussion so far indicates that the deposit-collecting banking sector, including state housing banks, is not a suitable business model for Islamic finance or housing finance. Another take from the discussion is that policy discourse is key to a healthy Islamic mortgage market rather than channeling more funds to the housing sector. Building more houses is not enough for sustainable cities, though.

The Role of Community Waqf in Real Estate Development

The system should produce more houses and provide necessary social infrastructure: education, health, water, and sanitation. The Islamic business model for the provision of social infrastructure services is Waqf. In the case of residential real estate development, schools, health clinics, and water and sanitation services should be managed by community Waqf (Diallo & Gundogdu, 2021). People living in the neighborhood should be responsible for these services. Hence, Waqf has a crucial role in providing social infrastructure in affordable housing.

> **Case Box 2.6: Drainage and Sanitation Project/Nigeria/Lagos**
> In June 1998, the World Bank Inspection Panel received a complaint from a local NGO from Nigeria on an IDA-financed drainage and sanitation project in Lagos. The NGO complained that the interest and the rights of the communities had and would be adversely affected due to the failure of IDAs to comply with the involuntary settlement, project monitoring and evaluation, gender dimension, and poverty reduction policies. It claimed that drainage channels became wastewater receptacles, which regularly flow

> into houses. People ended up being squatters and living too far from their employment.
>
> *Source* Shihata (2000)

The Islamic proposition to the social infrastructure development regarding the case above would be community Waqf. Without community ownership, which is possible with the Waqf business model, fatal flaws in project design, development, and sustainability would be a formidable challenge. Developing housing units without social infrastructure would undermine affordable housing efforts. Nevertheless, the business model selection in social infrastructure would determine the sustainability of living areas. In this regard, Waqf is an essential tool for attaining sustainable cities and communities defined in SDG-11. The role of Waqf is extensively discussed in Chapter 6.

REFERENCES

Barth, J. R., Caprio, G., & Levine, R. (2001). *Bank regulation and supervision: What works best?* (World Bank Policy Working Paper 2725).

Buckley, R. M., & Kalarickal, J. (2006). *Thirty years of World Bank shelter lending: What have we learned? Directions in development; infrastructure.* World Bank.

Buckley R., Chiquier, L., & Lea, M. (2009). *Housing finance and the economy in "housing finance policy in emerging markets."* World Bank.

Chiquier, L. (2009). Construction finance in emerging economies. In L. Chiquier & M. Lea (Eds.), *Housing finance policy in emerging markets.* World Bank.

De Soto, H. (2000). *The mystery of capital: Why capitalism triumphs in the west and fails everywhere else* (3rd ed.). A Member of the Perseus Books Group.

Diallo, A. T., & Gundogdu, A. S. (2021). *Sustainable development and infrastructure: An Islamic finance perspective.* Palgrave Macmillan.

Gundogdu, A. S. (2014). Two-step Murabaha in stock exchange as an alternative to commodity Murabaha for liquidity management. *International Journal of Financial Services Management, 7*(3–4), 268–285.

Gundogdu, A. S. (2016). Exploring novel Islamic finance methods in support of OIC exports. *Journal of Islamic Accounting and Business Research, 7*(2), 78–92.

Gundogdu, A. S. (2019). *A modern perspective of Islamic economics and finance.* Emerald Publishing.

Hasler, O., & Renaud, B. (2009). State housing banks. In L. Chiquier & M. Lea (Eds.), *Housing finance policy in emerging markets*. World Bank.

Kettell, B. (2011). *Case studies in Islamic banking and finance: Case questions & answers*. Wiley (UK).

Laidler, D. (1974). The 1974 report of the President's Council of Economic Advisers: The control of inflation and the future of the international monetary system. *American Economic Review, American Economic Association*, 64(4), 535–543.

Lea, M. (2009). Structure and evolution of housing finance system. In L. Chiquier & M. Lea (Eds.), *Housing finance policy in emerging markets*. World Bank.

Mason, D. (2004). *From building and loans to bail out: History of the American savings and loan industry 1831–1995*. Cambridge University Press.

Pasley, R. S. (2017). *Anatomy of a banking scandal: The keystone bank failure-harbinger of the 2008 financial crisis*. Routledge.

Renaud, B. (1999). The financing of social housing in integrating financial markets: A view from developing countries. *Urban Studies*, 36(4), 755–773. http://www.jstor.org/stable/43084626.

Rosly, S. A., & Sanusi, M. M. (1999). The application of Bay' Al-'Inah and Bay' Al-Dayn in Malaysian Islamic bonds: An Islamic analysis. *International Journal of Islamic Financial Services*, 1(2), 3–11.

Shihata, I. (2000). *The World Bank inspection panel*. Oxford University Press.

Yuksel, A. (2021). *Analysis of alternative capital sources for the financing of ventures: An approach within the framework of Islamic economics* (MA Thesis). Istanbul Zaim University.

CHAPTER 3

Food Security and Poverty

Assuring Supply-Side Stability

There have been competing views on food security: one side predicts food shortages with higher global prices, while others claim that progress in production technologies will match the demand with stable prices. However, the agreement is there on the inadequacy of food for the poor, especially in the world's poorest countries (Winkelmann, 1998).

Food security has multidimensions: availability, access to food, and sustainability (FAO, 1996). Availability would indicate food sufficiency and reliability, while access indicates equity. Hence, food security can be defined based on five factors: food sufficiency, reliability, autonomy, equity, and sustainability. A food security system should be designed to have the capacity to produce, store, and import or acquire. A state of sufficient food is when the supply of food meets the needs of all those who need it all the time. The food supply should be reliable so that the effect of cyclical, seasonal, and other variations in access to food is minimal.

A secure system should provide the maximum level of self-determination and autonomy to reduce vulnerability to market fluctuation and political and social pressure. The designed food security system should be equitable for all individuals. And most importantly, it should be environmentally and socially sustainable to ensure lasting results. Hence, while designing a food security system, we should not assume that a country's food security can be indicated by the per capita availability of

© The Author(s), under exclusive license to Springer Nature
Switzerland AG 2023
A. S. Gundogdu, *Food Security, Affordable Housing, and Poverty*,
Palgrave Studies in Islamic Banking, Finance, and Economics,
https://doi.org/10.1007/978-3-031-27689-7_3

aggregate food and that conventional economic policies nearly always contribute to greater food security. Even if we have enough food to feed the whole world, wrong policy choices will keep some social groups food insecure, which has been the case for several decades (South Center, 1997).

The conventional approach is that poverty is the reason for the lack of access to food.[1] The Islamic view is that people are deemed poor if they don't have access to food. These two views lead to a subtle difference: conventional economics understanding looks from the angle of the financial complex: having money is the panacea to all problems. This approach can be dangerous in the long run as the financial system can disconnect from the greenfield economy. Monetizing and commercializing customary institutions governing food distribution could exacerbate access to food for unfortunate people. The conventional finance approach opts for growth, by which the income of poor people supposedly increases with trickle-down, which can decrease the problem in the short run but lead to more significant long-term problems. Conventional economics understanding of poverty is income-based and assumes that income increase can sort out food security and poverty. However, no connection is proved between economic growth and poverty alleviation, nor the proposition that economic growth leads to income increase for all and, hence, poverty alleviation (Gundogdu, 2019). The Islamic view is more conducive to a holistic approach to eradicating the problem for good as it prioritizes equity.

The issue of agricultural land is a subject of a little bit different discussion than residential land. Managing agricultural land properly is the key to availability, hence, sustainable food security. Doomsday predictions on food shortages have not been realized. For instance, Borgstrom (1969) stated that the world is on the verge of famine never seen in history.[2] Other scholars have debunked this forecast, noting that our planet's land resources are enough if we look after them properly (Dyson, 1996; Higgins et al., 1982). In the same vein, some experts have warned that excessive input and high-yield methods could lead to environmental

---

[1] This is how World Food Summit in the document prepared for the global initiative on world food security matters identified the root cause.

[2] Islam does not accept the concept of "Too Many" and every human is valuable and has sustenance options available, yet, need to exert work-effort and use intellect.

pollution and soil degradation (Brown & Kane, 1995; Ehrlich et al., 1993) (Case Box 3.1).

> **Case Box 3.1: Rothamsted vs. Woburn**
> Rothamsted's long-term experiments concluded that high levels of inorganic fertilizer and pesticide inputs with improved crop varieties could increase the yield for more than a century and a half. However, that was true for Rothamsted was not true of nearby Woburn. The scientists who marked a substantial success in maintaining a high wheat and barley yield in Rothamsted failed in nearby Woburn, with lighter soil than Rothamsted, from 1877 to 1926. Powlson and Johnton (1994) rightly concluded about the Woburn experiment that seeking extrapolation results from the Broadbalk field of Rothamsted without factoring other climate and soil features of Woburn was unfortunate.
> *Source* Greenland et al. (1998)

There are also similar, to Rothamsted vs. Woburn case, long-term experiments, 10–30 years, in OIC member countries with the same result: maize grown at IITA in Nigeria and sorghum grown in the Sahel (Lal, 1992; Piere, 1992). It is also well established that crop production can change soil properties such as acidification, loss of organic matter, and removal of nutrients. For instance, wheat requires more water and takes more nutrients from the soil than sorghum, yet sorghum requires more herbicides and has a higher potential to give rise to erosion (Hendy et al., 1996). The improper use of fertilizers and pesticides would pollute soil and, more importantly, water resources. All these will add to the long-term problem of expensive remedies to treat soil degradation (Stoorvogel & Smalling, 1990).

Regardless of all the challenges noted above and well-structured scientific research, the superficial practice of excessive use of inputs in wastelands continued to culminate in today's food security debate. The aim should be to produce satisfactory crop yields without degradation of the soil. Sustainable soil management systems, over centuries, have been a tree, animal, and water-based, not fertilizers; as trees, animals, and water can effectively transfer nutrients to cultivated land while minimizing soil degradation (Young, 1989). However, they have occasionally failed in history, leading to civilization's collapse (Hillel, 1991). The solution to the occasional failure of sustainable methods is to ensure all the farmland across the globe is cultivated and a robust international trading system for agricultural commodities to support any region suffering from climate adversities. Climate change or hazard is not something new on this planet, as noted in the story of Yusuf/Joseph (PBUH), Surah 12: Ayah 43-49:

> [One day] the king said, 'I saw [in a dream] seven fat cows being devoured by seven lean ones, and seven green ears and [seven] others [that were] dry. O courtiers, give me your opinion about my dream if you can interpret dreams.' They said, '[These are] confused nightmares, and we do not know the interpretation of nightmares.' The one of the two who had been delivered, remembering [Joseph] after a long time: 'I will inform you of its interpretation; so let me go [to meet Joseph in prison].' 'Joseph,' [he said], 'O truthful one, give us your opinion concerning seven fat cows who are eaten by seven lean ones, and seven green ears and [seven] others dry, that I may return to the people so that they may know [the truth of the matter].' He said, 'You will sow for seven consecutive years. Then leave whatever [grain] you harvest in the ear, except a little you eat. Then there will come seven hard years which will eat up whatever you have set aside for them—all except a little which you preserve [for seed]. Then there will come a year wherein the people will be granted relief and provided with rains therein.
>
> —13: 43-49

Yusuf (PBUH), as a wise man, managed a warehousing system in Egypt to save not only Egypt but also neighboring countries that could survive on the stocks of Egypt with trading.

As it is, any climate hazard in extensive farmlands for which food supply is relied upon would cause a global-scale food crisis. This is why food production should not be delegated to certain countries or regions, but every part of the globe should be utilized. This will ensure that in case of climate adversary in one region, other regions not affected should continue with production. The solution for sustainable food security is to use minimum input across the global farmland based on water and soil realities of every single watershed rather than massive input use in mass-scale farming in a small portion of global land for food production (Diallo & Gundogdu, 2021). Nevertheless, this architecture should be supported with a robust international trade system, hence trade financing, for agricultural commodities.

SDGs and Food Security

Sustainability means assuring sufficient equity among social groups, meeting people's needs continuously, and ensuring autonomy for all social groups. Food security cannot be achieved in a vacuum. It needs an equitable solution in many other aspects of development. For instance, food security can be sustained if the natural ecosystem fails in the next generation due to heavy exploitation or destruction of institutions due to social unrest or war caused by inequality between social groups or countries. Producing enough food to feed the whole world statistically would not necessarily be equitable unless this leads to zero hunger.

The Sustainable Development Goals (SDGs), an expanded version of the Millennium Development Goals (MDGs) approved in 2000, were adopted in 2015 by the United Nations. They are a universal call to take action under 17 goals to achieve certain objectives by 2030 for global peace and prosperity. Precedent MDGs had eight goals to halve extreme poverty by 2015 and had a similar integrated approach to balance economic, environmental, and social sustainability (Table 3.1).

Compared to MDGs, SDGs appear to be more integrated and comprehensive. The results of MDGs are mixed, and it is debatable whether the MDGs efforts yielded the desired result. The reason might be that we keep having the same development intervention patterns and expecting different results. The challenges, however, suggest more revolutionary intervention is needed. The same end might be predicted for SDGs, though SDGs are much better detailed for an integrated approach (Table 3.2).

Table 3.1 The Millennium Development Goals (MDGs)		
	Goal 1	Eradicate extreme poverty and hunger
	Goal 2	Achieve universal primary education
	Goal 3	Promote gender equality and empower women
	Goal 4	Reduce child mortality
	Goal 5	Improve maternal health
	Goal 6	Combating HIV/AIDs, malaria, and other diseases
	Goal 7	Ensure environmental sustainability
	Goal 8	Develop a global partnership for the development

Source SDGs Fund

Table 3.2 Sustainable Development Goals (SDGs)

Goal 1	End poverty in all its forms everywhere
Goal 2	End hunger, achieve food security and improved nutrition, and promote sustainable agriculture
Goal 3	Ensure healthy lives and promote well-being for all at all ages
Goal 4	Ensure inclusive and equitable quality education and promote lifelong learning opportunities for all
Goal 5	Achieve gender equality and empower all women and girls
Goal 6	Ensure availability and sustainable management of water and sanitation for all
Goal 7	Ensure access to affordable, reliable, sustainable, and modern energy for all
Goal 8	Promote sustained, inclusive, and sustainable economic growth, full and productive employment, and decent work for all
Goal 9	Build resilient infrastructure, promote inclusive and sustainable industrialization, and foster innovation
Goal 10	Reduce inequality within and among countries
Goal 11	Make cities and human settlements inclusive, safe, resilient, and sustainable
Goal 12	Ensure sustainable consumption and production patterns
Goal 13	Take urgent action to combat climate change and its impacts
Goal 14	Conserve and sustainably use the oceans, seas, and marine resources for sustainable development
Goal 15	Protect, restore, and promote sustainable use of terrestrial ecosystems, sustainably manage forests, combat desertification, halt and reverse land degradation, and halt biodiversity loss
Goal 16	Promote peaceful and inclusive societies for sustainable development, provide access to justice for all, and build effective, accountable, and inclusive institutions at all levels
Goal 17	Strengthen the means of implementation and revitalize the global partnership for sustainable development

Source SDGs Fund

SDG-2 is about zero hunger and constitutes a broader food security ecosystem and sustainable agriculture. It identifies food security and sustainable agriculture as integral for grappling with hunger.

The traditional approach to food security is usually to have irrigation projects to address supply-side factors. In due course, irrigation projects have added drainage to lessen the side effects of irrigation, leading to sustainability issues. These projects could not yield long-run sustainable food security, regardless of short-term gains. In the recent literature, some solutions have been proposed to mitigate such. Instead of extensive irrigation and drainage projects, a small flexible infrastructure with crop selection based on the water realities of the region is proposed. Besides, local money-denominated input, post-harvest financing, and farmers' cooperatives to assure fair output prices and mitigate FX fluctuation risk have been proposed (Diallo & Gundogdu, 2021). The OIC food security programs, on the other hand, under the initiative propose conventional solutions at the OIC level[3]:

- Agricultural Production and Productivity
- Trade in Agricultural-Related Activities
- Partnerships Building and Resource Mobilization.

The thematic areas for input and output markets for strategic crops are identified for drought, lack of input financing, and post-harvest arrangements. The approach has two bottlenecks. Firstly, it assumes that conventional approaches can solve the problem. The conventional approaches have been there for decades in the context of other geographic clusters, yet they did not solve the food security issue. Second, even if everything is done correctly at the local, regional, or OIC level, unless there is a global policy discourse, particularly on commodity price formation, all the affords would be in vain. Having global policy discourse to ensure fair price formation and price stability for agricultural input and output/crops and preventing abrupt price fluctuation is key to ensuring steady agricultural endeavor and food security (Table 3.3).

Conventional intervention does not factor in the FX volatility risk of loans and price volatility risk in input and output markets. Proposed solutions in Table 3.3 are a way to mitigate, but not eliminate, such risks. Although such a ring-fencing mechanism may lessen the problem, long-run sustainability is only possible by addressing the root cause: commodity price fluctuation. The issue of speculation in global commodity exchange should be resolved to yield results for assuring food security. There is a need to discourage some financial speculators from ensuring food security. One way would be prohibiting the entry of non-producers and non-real buyers (those who do not buy products for their onward production) to bid and offer in the commodity exchange. The more holistic solution would be to dismantle non-Islamic commodity exchanges and replace

---

[3] Action Plan on the Recommendations of the 21st IDB Annual Symposium entitled: "Achieving Food Security in Member Countries in the Post-Crisis World."

Table 3.3 Causes and solutions

Cause	Conventional solution	Proposed solutions
Drought	Irrigation and drainage projects	Flexible small infrastructure with crop selection based on the water realities of the region (Diallo & Gundogdu, 2021)
Lack of agricultural input—FX loans, input prices	Input financing	Local money-denominated profit-loss sharing financing with microfinance (Gundogdu, 2018)
Post-harvest output prices	Cooperatives or local traders; post-harvest financing	Licensed warehouses and organized exchange/markets (Gundogdu, 2016)

Source The author

them with genuine Islamic versions. The very nature of the price mechanism suggests that there needs to be global action to assure fair price formation and avoid abrupt price movements. And this cannot be done at the national or OIC level but requires coordinated policy discourse between OIC and non-OIC countries. Global action is needed.

Food security is on the agenda of both regional and international organizations. It was the 35th session of the Organization of Islamic Cooperation Council (OIC) of the Council of Foreign Ministers (CFM), which called for intervention in the food security issue in June 2008. The resolution urged member countries and OIC institutions to unite their efforts to tackle the food crisis and develop joint agricultural projects to increase agricultural output with investment and transfer of cross-border knowledge.[4] In this pursuit, OIC CFM approved the establishment of the Islamic Organization of Food Security (IOFS) with the following aims and objectives[5]:

a. Provide expertise and technical know-how to member states on the various aspects of sustainable agriculture, rural development, food security, and biotechnology, including addressing the problems

---

[4] Based on SESRIC Report in the name of "Agriculture and Food Security in OIC Member Countries."

[5] On December 9–11, 2013 during the 40th session of the Council of Foreign Ministers held in Conakry, Guinea, 19 OIC Member States signed the IOFS Statute, which enters into full legal force after ratification by at least 10 signatures (IOFS Website).

posed by desertification, deforestation, erosion, and salinity, as well as providing social safety nets.
b. Assess and monitor, in coordination with member states, the food security situation in member states to determine and make necessary emergency and humanitarian assistance, including the creation of food security reserves.
c. Mobilize and manage financial and agricultural resources for developing agriculture and enhancing food security in member states.
d. Coordinate, formulate, and implement common agricultural policies, including exchanging and transferring appropriate technology and public food management system.

The aims and objectives focus on supply-side bottlenecks to increase output, which is reflected in IOFS strategic programs. The assumption is that by increasing agricultural output, particularly with irrigation infrastructure, the issue of food security would be solved automatically. However, the reality on the ground is much more convoluted.

Fi'sabilillah Spending

Islam encourages individuals to embrace an entrepreneurial spirit conducive to creating wealth. It also implores those that have succeeded in their endeavors to allocate a portion of what they earn to benevolent causes, as is clearly ordered by the Qur'an.[6] Several verses in the Qur'an clearly indicate that it is unacceptable to continuously accumulate wealth by failing to make provisions for those that need support.[7] For this reason, the issue of spending in the interest of benevolent causes is a crucial one in Islamic finance and economics. This topic has been the subject of discussion throughout Islamic history, as poverty is perceived similarly to challenges such as disbelief (*kufr*) in Islam. Muhammad (ﷺ)

---

[6] You can never have extended virtue and righteousness unless you spend part of what you dearly love for the cause of God. God knows very well whatever you spend for His cause (3:92).

[7] And let not those who [greedily] withhold what Allah has given them of His bounty ever think that it is better for them. Rather, it is worse for them. Their necks will be encircled by what they withheld on the Day of Resurrection. And to Allah belongs the heritage of the heavens and the earth. And Allah, with what you do, is [fully] Acquainted (3:180).

said: "O Allah! I seek refuge from disbelief (*kufr*) and poverty."[8] For this reason, the realities of the modern world call for a systematic explanation regarding the best spending structure for the cause of Allah (*fisabilillah*).

Confusion often exists regarding numerous important terms, including *Infaq*, *Sadaqah*, *Zakat*, and *Waqf* (Siddiqui, 2008). Such terms denote various kinds of spending and should not be used interchangeably. The Islamic perspective proposes that you begin with your community, which includes your immediate family (*infaq*), followed by your relatives and the neighborhood where you reside. The tern infaq relates to *nafaqa*. Every Muslim must work for and spend money on members of their family that do not qualify to receive Zakat. Specifically, parents must ensure that their children receive the education they need and have the assets required to meet their adult obligations toward their children and parents. If this is the case, parents will ensure that their children have the contemporary skills required to create value and make assistance available to their extended and immediate family members who require assistance. Sadaqah is a giver's charitable act when responding to an emergency. It differs from Zakat because it is not an obligation (Heck, n.d.). Therefore, Sadaqah is the mechanism that community members should use to deal with crises.

When a problem cannot be referred to as a once-off event but is ongoing, tools other than Sadaqah should be used to address it. The stubborn issues of hunger and poverty need to be addressed by creating a business environment that can economically empower people (Islamic microfinance), supported by Waqf and Zakat. Even though Zakat is generally perceived as a significant mechanism for addressing the issues of poverty and hunger, guidance from Muhammad (ﷺ) proposes that economic empowerment should be achieved by means other than Zakat. Undoubtedly, a great deal of confusion exists with regard to the various aspects of Zakat itself. The distinction between poverty and hunger is important in comprehending the role of Zakat in this context.

The manner in which Waqf and Zakat are presented in the literature as the solution to all challenges is irrational. Such representation shows a lack of understanding of the reality that different tools justify their presence by having different scopes. For instance, the social security net in Islam forms at the intersection between Waqf, Zakat, Sadaqah, and Infaq. In this arrangement, the security systems funded by tax revenues collected

---

[8] Sunan an-Nasa'i 5485.

by the government are not embraced. For instance, crowdfunding could be the method used for mobilizing Sadaqah resources under government supervision. The Islamic principle is based on the idea that resources should be gathered and immediately distributed from one account to the next without investing them in return. This will reduce the potential for corruption or misappropriation. In such an arrangement, the government's only responsibility is to supervise through regulation. Islam does not accept a situation where governments, religious community leaders, and institutions play a role in distributing charity for the sake of political agendas.

Zakat for Poverty Alleviation and Food Security

Zakat is not a long-term solution proposed for food security in Islam. The concept of Zakat often causes confusion. This results in Zakat funds often being used in a manner that defeats their intended purpose. Islam does not perceive Zakat as a tool for dealing with the challenge of individual poverty. Still, Zakat is a means for addressing the structural issues that lead to market inequalities and the wealth inequality this creates. The impact of Waqf and Zakat on alleviating poverty is indirect, with the goal of supporting systematic poverty alleviation efforts. This proposition is supported by historical accounts since the issue of poverty still exists in Muslim societies, notwithstanding continued Zakat collection (Hafidhuddin & Beik, 2010).

Notwithstanding sporadic periods of abundance, it has not been possible to get rid of visible poverty in the long run completely. For this reason, Islam proposes that poverty should be targeted directly through trade and entrepreneurship. To achieve this, vulnerable communities must be empowered economically. This is where Waqf and Zakat play a profound role in dealing with inequality, poverty, and hunger. Even then, the long-term goal is to create economic empowerment. Islam discourages a situation where those in need depend on charity, as illustrated in the hadith in Case Box 3.2.

Case Box 3.2: The Hadith Inspiring Economic Empowerment
A man of the Ansar community came to the Prophet (ﷺ) and begged him. (#1) He (the Prophet) asked: Have you nothing in your house? He (the man) replied: Yes, a piece of cloth, which we wear, or which we spread

> (on the ground), and a wooden bowl from which we drink water. (#2) He (the Prophet) said: Bring them to me. He (the man) then brought these items to him, and he (the Prophet) took them in his hands and asked the assembly of people: Who will buy these? A man said: I shall buy them for one dirham. He (the Prophet) asked twice or thrice: Who will offer more than one dirham? Another man said: I shall buy them for two dirhams. (#3) He (the Prophet) gave these to him and took the two dirhams and, giving them to the man of the Ansar, he said: Buy food with one of them and take it to your family, and buy an axe and bring it to me. (#4) He then brought it to him. The Prophet (peace be upon him) fixed a small branch of wood (as a handle) on it with his own hands (#5) and said: Go, cut and gather firewood and sell it, and do not let me see you for a fortnight. (#6) The man went away, cut and gathered firewood, and sold it. When he had earned ten dirhams, he came to him and bought a garment with some of them and food with the others. (#7) The Prophet (ﷺ) then said: This is better for you than begging, which should come as a spot on your face on the Day of Judgment.
>
> *Source* Gundogdu (2018)

From the above example of Muhammad (ﷺ), it can be noted that the Islamic approach to dealing with hunger is trade and entrepreneurship. Undoubtedly, the example in the hadith shares close similarities with modern Islamic principles regarding economic empowerment (Gundogdu, 2018). Preferably, the economic system should be designed to enable individuals to be independent and create a surplus. This can be achieved within an environment containing measures ensuring that the poor are not exploited. The system should ensure that prices are neither too high when someone is buying nor too low when selling so that those who produce food can continue doing so sustainably.

Vulnerable individuals need to be empowered to protect themselves from exploitation that could result from economies of scale. For this reason, Islam forbids Riba and ensures fair market price formation by prohibiting monopolies and systems that take advantage of those financially strained by offering below-market prices when purchasing items from them. The Islamic microfinance's empowerment approach is aimed at balancing economies of scale for vulnerable people by aggregating demands and supply to obtain the best price for them. Such an approach is also based on sharing profit or loss, which ensures that the system does not allow loan sharks. A careful analysis of this approach shows that it is not Zakat that will sustainably eradicate poverty but trade and entrepreneurship. However, even though Zakat can still play a supporting role, there is still a great deal of confusion regarding this concept (Kahf, 1995).[9]

It is vital to remain aware that Islam is not in support of a situation where the masses remain idle, expecting to receive money from governments or the wealthy because it hurts dignity. For instance, when people depend on government, support of the charity of the wealthy tends to be highly obedient, even when their society, government and wealthy minority are plagued by malevolence and impose oppression. For this reason, economic empowerment within Islamic microfinance should be the primary element in alleviating food insecurity, hunger, and poverty. This implies that economic empowerment programs should desist from using the resources of Zakat and Waqf. Instead, they should develop economically viable programs to ensure added value. Zakat has direct societal effects on inequality and hunger in transition. As a business model, Waqf is aimed at operating social infrastructure. However, corporate Waqf and temporary cash Waqf models can be employed for mobilizing resources to provide social infrastructure. Waqf and Zakat both have distinctive, valuable, and indistinctive roles. Nonetheless, for long-term and sustainable results, poverty and hunger alleviation and guarantee of security should focus on economic empowerment.

---

[9] The confusion relates to the following major aspects of *zakat*:
  a. Who should give *zakat* (Muzakki)?
  b. Who should be beneficiaries of Zakat (Mustahiq)?
  c. Who should distribute *zakat*?
  d. Where should *zakat* be distributed?
  e. Cash vs. in-cash-kinds of *zakat* allocation.
  f. Calculation of *zakat* based on market value net-worth vs. income generated from assets.
  g. Can we accumulate *zakat* funds and use return from investments as proceeds for distribution?

Economic Empowerment Programs

Economic empowerment has been applied in several countries with positive results.[10] As an approach, it is less risky but more profitable for all parties, whether one is looking at communities, fund users, or fund producers. Economic empowerment is effective at battling poverty and facilitating social development and security because it introduces social projects that are more resistant and stable. The concept is based on the understanding that fundamental hurdles need to be lifted to assist in eradicating poverty, ensuring food security, and getting rid of hunger. This will also ensure that the poor will be integrated into the value chain to become independent. Consequently, economic empowerment based on Islamic microfinance is based on the understanding that the needs of low-income groups are multidimensional. This implies that financing is just one facet of poverty. Poverty is seen as having more to do with the inability to take advantage of supportive infrastructures, fair price information, networks for market access, economies of scale, and project opportunities.[11]

Notwithstanding the reality that economic empowerment is an Islamic microfinance program, it is not known as Islamic microfinance for several reasons. One is that its philosophy is based on the need to deal with challenges linked to microfinance, whether Islamic or conventional. It seeks to address a situation where microfinance institutions (MFIs) often leave more people poor because their businesses are run for profit only. To accomplish their objective, microfinance institutions take advantage of the poor by lending money without considering the value that will be added and driving competition in communities and taking advantage of

---

[10] The Islamic Development Bank's results have been impressive for Palestine, Sudan, Yemen, Kazakhstan, and Benin.

[11] A supportive infrastructure involves the creation and supply of economic zones, industrial zones, warehouses, generators, water purification units, incubators, packaging centers, laboratories, and other projects that cannot be provided by one initiative but can be achieved within the framework of unions, cooperatives, and solidarity groups. One of the objectives of these supportive projects is to ensure that initiatives for the economic empowerment of the poor have the same chance of success as large and medium enterprises in the private sector.

the fact that the financially illiterate do not understand the way finances are calculated.[12]

To create value for the poor, the main focus of the economic empowerment concept is on value chains and boosting cooperation among groups as opposed to competition. From experience, it can be noted that sectors like agriculture facilitate value addition. On the other hand, informal urban employment, which drives zero-sum game competition, does not. Where MFIs see the beneficiaries of microfinance as business partners, purchase agricultural inputs for all farmers at a discounted price, and take the role of off-takers when the harvest arrives so that they can sell the produce from the farmers in high volumes for higher prices. Such intervention ensures that farmers are no longer prone to exploitation. Consequently, it can be posited that participating in microfinance programs can leave farmers better-off.

The concept employed also has additional benefits like bulk storage and training. For this reason, it is suggested that this model be extended to other supportive infrastructures to support value chains. Moreover, Zakat can support microfinance programs, so farmers do not resort to microfinance loans for food. This is because the use of microfinance loans for food is one of the reasons such interventions often do not succeed. Because low-income households often approach microfinance loans because they are desperate, they usually default. This results in them being punished for the rest of their lives by microfinance companies blacklisting them and ensuring that they never get a loan again.

The challenges met by low-income households concerning obtaining financing could be alleviated by the introduction of economic empowerment. Zakat money can be used if required to ensure that farmers can access food and ensure that the loans these farmers receive are used only for their business activities. Nonetheless, Zakat must be used for its traditional context and not as a way of bailing out farmers in distress.[13] From experience, it has been noted that farmers who eventually get to know

---

[12] Sinclair, H. (2012). *Confessions of a microfinance heretic: How microlending lost its way and betrayed the poor*. Berrett Koehler Publishers.

[13] Kahf, M. (2004). *Shari'ah and historical aspects of zakat and Waqf* (Background paper prepared for the Islamic Research and Training Institute, Islamic Development Bank

that the funds allocated to them are linked to Zakat, or there is potential that Zakat would be used to bail them out when in distress tend to default or present a default case.[14]

An economic empowerment fund introduces resource mobilization in cash Waqf format.[15] In that format, resources are mobilized under an economic empowerment fund before they are invested for profit in microfinance. This aims to create a snowball effect that facilitates access to finance for low-income individuals. The format ensures protection through micro Takaful, fair harvest prices, and discounted inputs. These low-income individuals become business partners that can introduce value if adequately directed and provide equal opportunities to compete with considerably bigger businesses. Return on investment of cash Waqf funds from the farmers can be used for the provision of social infrastructure.

The comparison between Islamic microfinance and traditional microfinance is presented in Table 3.4.

Establishing economic empowerment funds aims to enter into investment partnerships with low-income individuals commercially. From this perspective, the concept is comparable to the development of Waqf and endowment with a high possibility for improving social welfare. Typically, these generous endowments are in the form of real estate or land. Nonetheless, cash Waqf is also permitted. This Waqf is known as cash Waqf when it is established by cash endowment to support the poor.[16] Development Waqf differs from traditional cash Waqf. The difference is that the former is invested in the organized sector for bankable projects, with the returns used for the poor. In contrast, the latter is invested in a portfolio of bankable and un-bankable projects from the poor's unorganized sectors.

---

[14] In the case of microfinance provided by the Islamic Development Bank through the Bank of Khartoum, the initial success of agricultural microfinance faded once the farmers were informed that the resource was zakat.

[15] Cizakca, Ahmed, and Kahf proposed the use of the cash Waqf concept for Islamic MFIs. More recently, Haneef et al. developed an integrated Waqf-based Islamic microfinance design in Bangladesh as a means to alleviate poverty.

[16] Kahf, M. (2000). al Waqf al Islami, Tatawwuruh, Idaratuh, Tanmiyatuh (Islamic Waqf, its growth, management, and development). Damascus: Dar al Fikr. Kahf, M. (2004). Shari'ah and historical aspects of zakat and awqaf. Background paper prepared for the Islamic Research and Training Institute, Islamic Development Bank

Table 3.4 Classic microfinance vs. Islamic microfinance based on the economic empowerment concept

Classic microfinance	Microfinance based on the approach of economic empowerment
The fundamental need is for finance	There are several basic needs: access to project opportunities, partnerships, basic infrastructures, financing, and markets
The marginalized or low-income individual is a credit borrower	The marginalized or low-income individual is a business partner with great potential for generating wealth
Gains from transactions with low-income individuals are made even when this leads to their suffering	The practice followed is that of participatory finance: gains are made from transactions with low-income individuals but solidarity with the latter remains Ethical finance is practiced; thus, ethical rules are followed
Individual micro-project microfinancing	Micro-projects, medium projects, integrated projects, small and medium-sized enterprises, large projects, micro/small/large financing
MFIs undertake the financing	MFIs are socioeconomic actors
MFIs operate with short-term clients	MFIs conduct business with their clients in the short, medium, and long terms depending on the projects' natures
The clients manage their projects	MFIs support customers with the management of their projects until the customers become autonomous
MFIs manage the financing	MFIs manage the value chains in collaboration with a network of specialized partners
Microcredit	Financial engineering with different appropriate Islamic financing methods that ensure projects' profitability

Source Gundogdu (2018)

When such a direct investment approach to invest with smallholder farmers is embraced, the impact on food security and hunger is exponentially increased. The reason for this is that the returns from these types of investments also cater to communities in rural areas as they will be used for the provision of social infrastructure. Resources from the economic empowerment fund consist of Zakat, corporate social responsibility programs, international financial institutions, national financial institutions, donor countries, and development Waqf paid-in capital.

From the point of view based on Islamic principles, Zakat will not be used in such projects because it is required to be a direct transfer of wealth. For this reason, Zakat has to be explicitly transferred from the rich to the poor.

THE ISSUE OF AGRICULTURAL PRICES

The issue of food security has been on the agenda of international organizations for some time. However, no decisive results have been achieved yet. This could be attributed to the price volatility of agricultural inputs and outputs. International food prices are volatile because demand for foods is inelastic in the face of supply fluctuation, making the sector attract speculators. As indicated in Fig. 3.1, with the highest food prices, it is not surprising that food security issues were on the agenda in July 2008, coinciding with record-high food prices.

It suggests a need to question traditional supply-side approaches/projects' viability to attain food security. Decades of both national governments and international development agencies' efforts with classical agricultural development projects based on irrigation and drainage have not yielded sustainable food security in the long run,

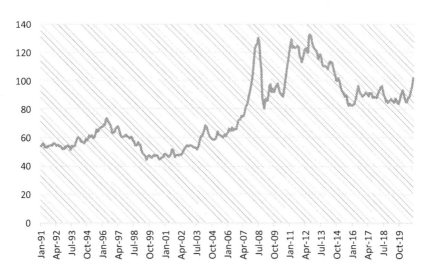

Fig. 3.1 Commodity food price index (*Source* Index Mundi)

but short-term gains exacerbated long-term results. In new literature, proposals also appear to suggest risk mitigation rather than addressing the root causes.

Increasing output is possible for a short period, yet lasting results often prove challenging in the long run. Market and price formation dynamics are ignored due to the heavy focus on mass-scale production approaches. Forty percent of the agricultural output is produced in only 6.5 percent of irrigated areas worldwide (Diallo & Gundogdu, 2021). Such reliance is very dangerous. It is possible that a natural catastrophe could befall this limited agricultural land. Therefore, the sustainable way is to have every corner of the world cultivated by smallholder farmers based on crops selected per the soil and water reality of their land. However, this is a substantial shift from mass-scale farming to small-scale farming and requires safeguarding small farming.

The traditional approaches are not farmer-centric. On the ground, the farmers very often end up not being able to prepare themselves for the next harvest in case output prices drop drastically as they cannot prepare for the next harvest. The cycle of input and output often gets broken in price volatility. Mass-scale investment with foreign exchange loans at price booms end up in misery once the prices plummet. For instance, in 2011, several cotton agricultural development projects were approved by Multilateral Development Banks (MDBs) based on the prevailing cotton prices, as indicated in Fig. 3.2.

Farmers and countries that received massive FX loans based on March 2011 cotton prices had inflicted huge losses after prices dropped from US\$ 5 to US\$ 2.5 from March to September 2011. And was the case with the Kandi-Segbana-Nigeria Border Road Project, which was signed in January 2011 by the government of Benin. The case is presented in Case Box 3.3.

Case Box 3.3: Kandi-Segbana-Nigeria Border Road Project
The transport project involved a total of US\$ 76.8 million with the aim of connecting the rural population to markets. The assumptions of the project appraisal were based on high cotton prices, which was the main factor in paying back FX loans received.

Cotton as a cash crop is assumed to be an integral part of food security. With FX earning from cotton export, sub-Saharan African countries can import agricultural input. In this regard, smallholders allocate some part

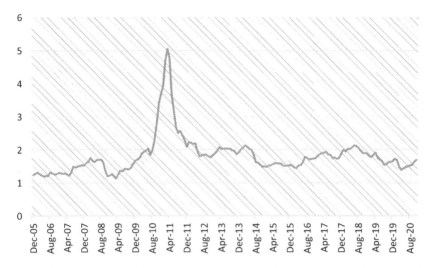

Fig. 3.2 Cotton monthly price—US dollars per kilogram (*Source* Index Mundi)

> of their land for cash crops next to staples. However, volatility in input and output prices put the government in a difficult position regarding paying back FX loans to invest in roads, irrigation and drainage, and cotton cooperatives. The governments were affected by input price volatility and FX volatility. Hence, the approach to having cash crops could not yield the desired result for food security in the region.
> *Source* OPEC Fund

Centralized planned mass-agricultural production by the state failed in the long run. This is evidenced by the communist experience. Delegating food production to a big corporation, a business model of capitalism, may enhance food production in the short run. Still, it would not lead to sustainable food security in the long term as it undermines food security. It also puts countries in a situation where they are subject to the dictates of other nations, big corporations, or international organizations. Bestowing price formation to very few countries and corporations would not lead to fair price formation but to oligopol prices. As mentioned before, relying on a handful of countries or corporations is problematic, even if they do not exploit their dominant positions. In case of natural disasters in certain regions, the whole world would end up with food insecurity.

Relying on smallholders in each country has been a sustainable business model throughout history. The focus should be on providing an enabling environment for smallholders and ensuring specific agricultural production in each country. However, development efforts to support smallholders with agricultural development projects meet challenges related to external factors such as price volatility and the burden of FX loans. The issue of FX loans, in a way, shapes countries' crop preferences. For instance, Burkina Faso adopted GMO cotton seeds from 2008 to 2011. Coincidently, these were cotton price boom years until 2011 to enhance FX earning capacity. However, this resulted in cotton farmers becoming destitute (Dowd-Uribe, 2014). Smallholder preference appears to be different from policymakers' as they are more inclined to produce short-cycled and easy-to-sell products. FX loans make governments urge farmers to grow risky products, even if without their consent. The backbone of conventional interventions: irrigation infrastructure projects with FX-denominated loans exacerbates food security standing. Public authorities force farmers to cultivate cash crops to repay FX-denominated loans, while farmers prefer short-cycle, easy-to-sell produce to repay FX loans.

Irrigation projects with FX loans lead to a side effect of underground water level increase. Hence, to cope with the side effects of irrigation projects, drainage projects with more FX loans were introduced. However, even integrated irrigation and drainage projects are at risk. That is, the international infrastructure projects to underpin the supply side do not help food security in the long run. Another way around, these projects pile FX debt in the country with no real progress in food security for the countries in the long run (Diallo & Gundogdu, 2021). As a different account for FX-denominated loans, project finance and FX-denominated input financing loans are problematic. At times, harvest prices may not cover input costs due to commodity price fluctuations. The farmer's yield is not enough to pay back input financing. A more sustainable solution might be to decrease input use in production with local solutions and local loans with microfinance based on the profit-loss-sharing business model, aka economic empowerment (Gundogdu, 2018).

Avoiding FX debt for infrastructure and input financing may abate FX risk for the farmers. However, the boom-and-bust cycle for commodity and agricultural input prices is an area that should be extensively discussed in global policymaking. Financialization of commodities in organized exchange gives rise to such boom-and-bust cycles, which may benefit financial speculators, who are neither actual sellers nor buyers but inflict heavy losses on global food security efforts. In this regard, having proper storage facilities for farmers to plan their sales in harvest surplus with organized exchange to assure fair price formation for actual sellers and buyers who are in the agriculture business is key to assure smallholder farmers' financial health, hence, sustainable food security (Gundogdu, 2016).

There is no long-lasting solution as long as there is no global policy to ensure price stability for input and output markets for agricultural commodities. Elimination of risk requires a global policy discourse to inhibit speculation in agricultural commodity prices:

- The price fluctuation in input and output markets should be stopped. This can be done through global partnerships. The speculators should not be allowed to bet on price movements with Shari'ah non-compliant options and futures. Noting that fair price formation is the central issue of Islamic economics with the ban of Nahr, Ihtikar, Najash, etc.
- If we can stop Shari'ah non-compliant options and futures, 50% of the problem will be resolved.
- Stop big irrigation projects (dams particularly) and mass chemical inputs; instead, adopt crop selection based on soil and water realities of the region to decrease fertilizer and pesticides. This would mean changing the business model from mass-scale farming to smallholder farming. Historically, smallholder farming has proved to be sustainable in the long run.
- There is no comparative advantage in agriculture; every country should produce as much as it can so long as crops fit their soil and water. The world cannot rely on a handful of countries for agricultural products, which is very risky in the case of climate or political adversities.

At both OIC and global levels, it is assumed that food security can be attained with projects targeting supply-side issues, particularly irrigation and drainage infrastructure development. There is also a need to shift focus to input financing and post-harvest arrangements. In this case, it is vital to avoid extensive irrigation and drainage infrastructure but have flexible and small irrigation schemes; proper crop selection based on water and soil realities of the geography. Besides, FX loans should be avoided in infrastructure project finance and input financing. Most importantly, a proper post-harvest market should assure farmers' fair returns.

Even if everything is done correctly in the locality, as long as speculation in agricultural commodities prices persists globally, the efforts to establish food security will not yield a sustainable result, bankrupting farmers. If speculators in commodity exchange plummet output prices during the post-harvest area, all efforts would be lost. In such an event, farmers would find themselves in trouble with meeting their obligations in relation to their local loans, which may not be paid due to low prices.

Speculating and financial speculators in global commodity exchange should be eliminated if we want food security. One way to do so would be prohibiting the entry of non-producers and non-real buyers who do not buy products for their onward production but bid and offer in the commodity exchange. The more holistic solution would be to dismantle non-Islamic commodity exchanges and replace them with genuine Islamic versions. Again, the very nature of the price mechanism suggests that there needs to be global action to assure fair price formation and avoid abrupt price movements. And this cannot be done at a national or the OIC level but requires coordinated policy discourse between OIC and non-OIC countries. Sustainable food security cannot be achieved locally, nationally, and regionally. It requires a global partnership.

Post-Harvest Losses and the Role of Warehousing

Losing produced food is unfortunate due to post-harvest bottlenecks. A comprehensive post-harvest system can identify bottlenecks and mitigate food loss. A decrease in post-harvest losses would enhance food availability and reduce food prices. The issue is more severe in case the food is perishable. For instance, reducing post-harvest losses for fruits and vegetables from between 20 and 40% to 10% would substantially increase the availability and reduce the price. Hence, a focus is needed to identify the weak links in the supply chain. Technological progress in information and communication technologies supports the development of optimal systems to reduce post-harvest losses (Gill & Poulter, 1998).

The key to developing a post-harvest system is identifying the critical point in the supply chain. It is warehousing. Effective warehousing historically has been the major contributor to food security, as the case presented in the story of Yusuf (PBUH) shows. Effective warehousing would not only reduce post-harvest losses but also help stabilize agricultural prices. Price stability is the core of agricultural policy because agricultural production depends on environmental conditions and weather that are inherently unstable (FAO, 1985). Countries with quality warehousing systems with laboratory testing capacity are in much better shape from a food security perspective (Kayada & Gundogdu, 2021). An adequate warehousing infrastructure enables the channeling of funds for the agricultural sector, as warehouse receipts can be used as collateral for financial institutions.

Proper storage decreases the losses, and grading with laboratory testing increases the value of the crop. Grading and quality storage transform crops into commodities, substantially increasing salability. Warehousing attached with laboratories for standard and conformity assessment and grading capacity paves the way for international trade. The obtained foreign currency can be used to procure agricultural inputs.

International Trade of Agricultural Commodities

Food security has five dimensions: food sufficiency, autonomy, reliability, equity, and sustainability. Sufficiency is related to the production and supply of food, while reliability is the provision of adequate food during cyclical or climatic variations. That is why Islam champions international trade, as it will enhance sufficiency and reliability. With international trade, maximum output with minimum input can be made available at much lower prices. And countries have important possibilities to decrease the adverse effects of cyclical and climatic variations.

The discussion above defines a market structure in which many smallholder farmers should produce agricultural products based on their geography's soil and water realities with minimum input. The problem of sporadic insufficiency would not be resolved with such an approach. International trade would bring about abundance as people could access different varieties. However, cross-border trade would still have its peculiarities: trade protection and facilitation. Many countries should be expected to impose tariff and non-tariff barriers to bar substitute products from abroad from flooding the market. For instance, naturally, a rice-producing country may end up with rural derogation in case of cheap wheat flooding into the country and forcing smallholder farmers to abstain from traditional rice cultivation. In case of the threat of substitute products, it is acceptable for each country to manage its tariff regime, noting that this should be allowed only in the case of substitute crops. Non-tariff barriers should be eliminated with trade facilitation efforts. The critical elements of a global effort for agricultural crop trade facilitation would be:

Standard and conformity assessment tests: The products in an agricultural field have little financial value unless graded, quality certified, and stored in a licensed warehouse. The grading, certification of quality, and warehousing process would turn the crop into a commodity. The process substantially increases the product's value and makes it readily tradable and financeable. Mainly, converting crops into electronic warehouse receipts would substantially increase the value for smallholder farms and facilitate financing and cross-border trade. However, many countries lack standard and conformity assessment tests and licensing warehousing (Gundogdu, 2012). The issue can be addressed with sanitary and phytosanitary capacity building and mutual recognition agreements to facilitate testing of other countries. Hence, particular emphasis should be given to capacity development under the aid-for-trade initiative.

Customs Valuation: Once a crop is commodified with grading, certification, and warehousing, the price information can be easily revealed. The price information is key for customs authorities attempting to levy a tariff. Although Islam forbids tax, particularly transaction taxes, using a tariff to protect local agricultural production against possible substitution effects, which could adversely affect local agricultural production, is acceptable (Gundogdu, 2019). Each country can have its parameters to allow the desired level of entry of foreign agricultural commodities to its territory based on the long-term best interest of its population. Indeed, such country-specific trade policy is a need to safeguard smallholder farmers. The issue of under-invoicing would undermine such safeguard efforts. The best solution is to have a globally integrated single window that is an electronic solution to many customs. However, these systems are not communicating with each other on a global scale. Should these single windows be integrated globally, sanitary and phytosanitary testing, invoice, certificate of origin, payment, and other needed documents can be streamlined from the country of origin to the country of destination and administrated by WTO Agreement on Customs Valuation Agreement and WTO Agreement on Sanitary and Phytosanitary Measures (Gundogdu, 2011).

The WTO Agreement on Agriculture introduced the inaugural international rules for international trade. Since it was negotiated, the agreement has been fundamental to the controversy around the impact and purpose of the WTO itself. This commentary focuses on a complete legal analysis of the obligations imposed by the agreement on WTO members and the intricate past relating to the negotiation, revision, and controversy relating to how it would impact international development. The commentary is structured around the three areas of reform initiated by the agreement: export competition and market access. Furthermore, the agreement provides a wide-ranging analysis of practical provisions and the disagreements related to these three areas. The agreement also places the identified provisions against background before the promulgation of the WTO regulation. It contains an analysis of the "Peace clause" operation, evaluates the effect on developing economies, and examines the process of restructuring subsidies in the domestic market. This is one of the main challenges the WTO is grappling with (McMahon, 2006).

The WTO Agreement on Agriculture's preamble states, "Noting that commitments under the reform program should be made equitable among all Members, regarding non-trade concerns, including food security." Implementing the notion of "Comparative Advantage" in the trade of agricultural commodities would undermine food security. Perhaps, that is why the WTO Agreement on Agriculture recognized the food security concern.

The well-designed international trade system can achieve the desired outcome of assuring the livelihood of smallholder farmers by enabling sustainable local production while allowing managed imports to ensure abundance. WTO Agreement on Agriculture, with other WTO Agreements under WTO multilateralism, can fit the bill. However, international trade necessitates substantial financing to move agricultural commodities across borders, which is needed to avoid the collapse of countries during bad years. The next chapter focus on Islamic cross-border trade finance.

References

Ahmed, H. (2004). *Role of Zakat and Awqaf in poverty alleviation*. Islamic Research and Training Institute, Islamic Development Bank Group.

Ahmed, H. (2011). Waqf-based microfinance: Realizing the social role of Islamic finance. In K. Monzer & M. M. Siti (Eds.), *Essential readings in contemporary Waqf issues* (p. 205239). CERT.

Al-Qaradawi, Y. (1994). *Fiqh al-Zakat*. Maktabah Wahbah.
Anwar, M. (1995). Financing socio-economic development with Zakat funds. *Journal of Islamic Economics*, 4(1–2).
Borgstrom, G. (1969). *Too many—A study of the earth's biological limitations*. Macmillan.
Brown, L. R., & Kane, H. (1995). *Full house: Reassessing the earth's population-carrying capacity*. Earthscan Publication.
Cizakca, M. (2000). *History of philanthropic foundations*. Bogazici University Press.
Cizakca, M. (2004, March 1–3). *Cash Waqf as alternative to NBFIs Bank*. Paper presented at the International Seminar on Nonbank Financial Institutions: Islamic Alternatives, jointly organized by Islamic Research and Training Institute, Islamic Development Bank, and Islamic Banking and Finance Institute Malaysia, Kuala Lumpur.
Dayson, T. (1996). *Population and food*. Routledge.
Diallo, A. T., & Gundogdu, A. S. (2021). *Sustainable development and infrastructure: An Islamic finance perspective*. Palgrave Macmillan.
Dowd-Uribe, B. (2014). Engineering yields and inequality? How Institutions and Agro-Ecology Shape Bt Cotton Outcomes in Burkina Faso. *Geoforum*, 53, 161–171. https://doi.org/10.1016/j.geoforum.2013.02.010
Ehrlich, P. R., Ehrlich, A. H., & Daily, G. C. (1993). Food security, population, and the environment. *Population and Development Review*, 19, 1–32.
FAO. (1985). *Agricultural price policies issues and proposals* (FAO Agricultural and Social Development Series, No: 42: Italy).
FAO. (1996, February). *World food submit (Rome, 13–17 November 1996)* (Basic Information, No. 5, Rome).
Gill, M., & Poulter, N. (1998). A systems perspective on postharvest losses. In J. C. Waterlow, D. G. Armstrong, L. Fowden, & R. Riley (Eds.), *Feeding a world population of more than eight billion people*. Oxford University Press.
Greenland, D. J., Gregory, P. J., & Nye, P. H. (1998). Land resources and constraints to crop production. In J. C. Waterlow, D. G. Armstrong, L. Fowden, & R. Riley (Eds.), *Feeding a world population of more than eight billion people*. Oxford University Press.
Gundogdu, A. S. (2011). Determinants of OIC countries' custom revenue vis-à-vis implementation of WTO customs valuation agreement. *Journal of Economic Cooperation*, 32(3), 39–64.
Gundogdu, A. S. (2012). *Developing Islamic finance opportunities for trade financing: Essays on Islamic trade vis-à-vis the OIC ten-year programme of action* [Ph.D. dissertation, Durham University, UK].
Gundogdu, A. S. (2016, December). Islamic electronic trading platform on organized exchange. *Borsa Istanbul Review*, 16(4), 249–255.

Gundogdu, A. S. (2018). An inquiry into Islamic finance from the perspective of sustainable development goals. *European Journal of Sustainable Development*, 7(4), 381. https://doi.org/10.14207/ejsd.2018.v7n4p381
Gundogdu, A. S. (2019). *A modern perspective of Islamic economics and finance*. Emerald Publishing.
Hafidhuddin, D., & Beik, I. (2010). Zakat development: Indonesia's experience. *Jurnal Ekonomi Islam Al Infaq*, 1(1), 1–5.
Haneef, M. A., Pramanik, A. H., Mohammed, M. O., Amin, M. F. B., & Muhammad, A. D. (2015). Integration of Waqf-Islamic microfinance model for poverty reduction: The case of Bangladesh. *International Journal of Islamic and Middle Eastern Finance and Management*, 8(2), 246–270. https://doi.org/10.1108/IMEFM-03-2014-0029
Hashim, M. A. (2010, 16–17 February). *The corporate Waqf: A Malaysian experience in building sustainable business capacity*. Paper delivered at Dubai International Conference on Endowments. Dubai, United Arab Emirates. https://www.unescwa.org/events/dubai-international-conference-endowm ents-innovative-sources-finance-small-and-medium-sized. Accessed 13 January 2019.
Hassan, M. K. (2010, 6–7 January). *An integrated poverty alleviation model combining Zakat, Awqaf, and micro-finance*. Seventh International Conference: The Tawhidi Epistemology: Zakat and Waqf Economy. Bangi, Malaysia. http://www.ukm.my/hadhari/publication/proceedings-of-seventh-internati onal-conference-the-tawhidi-epistemology-zakat-and-waqf-economy. Accessed on 13 January 2019.
Heck, P. L. (2018). *Taxation in Encyclopaedia of the Qurʾān* (J. Dammen McAuliffe, General Ed.). Georgetown University Press. Consulted online on 12 December 2018. https://doi.org/10.1163/1875-3922_q3_EQCOM_0 0199
Hendy, C. R. C., Kleih, U., & Crawshaw, R. (1996). *Interaction between livestock production systems and the environment* (Global Impact Donor Demand for Feed Concentrates). Natural Resource Institutes, Chatham.
Heyneman, S. P. (2004). *Islam and social policy*. Vanderbilt University Press.
Higgins, G. M., Kassam, L. Naiken, L., Fischer, G., & Shah, M. M. (1982). *Potential population-supporting capacities of lands in the developing world*. FAO.
Hillel, D. (1991). *Out of the earth*. The University of California.
Johnston, A. E., & Powlson, D. S. (1994). The setting-up, conduct and applicability of long-term, continuing field experiments in agricultural research. In D. J. Greenland & I. Szabolcs (Eds.), *Soil resilence and substainable land use* (pp. 395–421). CAB International.
Kahf, M. (1989). Zakat: Unresolved issues in the contemporary Fiqh. *IIUM Journal of Economics and Management*, 2(1).

Kahf, M. (1995). *Fiqh Al-Zakah* (as translated from the original work of Y. Qaradhawi). Center for Research in Islamic Economics, King Abdulaziz University.

Kahf, M. (2000). *Al Waqf al Islami, Tatawwuruh, Idaratuh, Tanmiyatuh (Islamic Waqf, its growth, management, and development)*. Dar al Fikr.

Kahf, M. (2004). *Shari'ah and historical aspects of Zakat and Awqaf* (Background paper prepared for the Islamic Research and Training Institute, Islamic Development Bank).

Kayada, A., & Gundogdu, A. S. (2021). Fundamentals of novel Islamic monetary system for the contemporary age. *Journal of Islamic Economics and Finance, 7*(2), 293–322.

Kister, M. J. (1965). The market of the prophet. *Journal of the Economic and Social History of the Orient, 8*(3), 272–276.

Kuran, T. (2001). The provision of public goods under Islamic Law: Origins, impact, and limitations of the Waqf system. *Law & Society Review, 35*(4), 841–898.

Lal, R. (1992). *Tropical agricultural hydrology and sustainability of agricultural systems—A ten-year watershed project in Southwestern Nigeria*. Ohio State University Press.

McMahon, J. (2006). *The WTO agreement on agriculture: A commentary* (number 9780199275687). OUP Catalogue, Oxford University Press.

Muhtada, D. (2008). The role of Zakat organization in empowering the peasantry: A case study of the Rumah Zakat Yogyakarta Indonesia. In M. Obaidullah & S. Abdullateef (Eds.), *Islamic finance for micro and medium enterprises*. IRTI, Islamic Development Bank.

Obaidullah, M. (2013). *Awqaf development and management*. Islamic Research and Training Institute, Islamic Development Bank.

Obaidullah, M. (2016a). Revisiting estimation methods of business Zakat and related tax incentives. *Journal of Islamic Accounting and Business Research, 7*(4), 349–364.

Obaidullah, M. (2016b). *Zakat management for poverty alleviation*. Islamic Research and Training Institute.

Obaidullah, M., & Abdullateef, S. (2011). *Islamic finance for micro and medium enterprises*. IRTI.

Piere, C. J. M. G. (1992). *Fertility of soils: A future for farming in the West African Savannah*. Springer Verlag.

Salehi, D. (2017). Poverty and income inequality in the Islamic Republic of Iran. *Revue Internationale Des Etudes Du Développement, 2017*(1), 1113–1136.

Siddiqui, A. (2008). *Qur'anic keywords*. The Islamic Foundation.

Sinclair, H. (2012). *Confessions of a microfinance heretic: How micro-lending lost its way and betrayed the poor*. Berrett Koehler Publishers.

South Centre. (1997). *Universal food security: Issues for the South*. South Centre.

Stoorvogel, J. K., & Smalling, M. A. (1990). *Assessment of the soil-nutrient depletion in Africa* (Report 28). Winand Staring Centre.

Winkelmann, D. L. (1998). Productivity, poverty alleviation, and food security. In J. C. Waterlow, D. G. Armstrong, L. Fowden, & R. Riley (Eds.), *Feeding a world population of more than eight billion people*. Oxford University Press.

Young, A. (1989). *Agroforestry for soil conversation*. CAB International.

CHAPTER 4

Financing the Trade of Agricultural Commodities

Assuring demand-side stability

To assure demand-side stability and move commodities forward across borders, trade finance is much needed. However, the issue of risk associated with agricultural commodity finance is challenging. Hence, many financial institutions shun proper engagement in the sector. Proper engagement means taking collateral in a way that aligns with the transaction. For instance, asking for mortgages as collateral for agricultural commodity trade is inappropriate. This is because it fuels real estate prices as it gets an additional feature of financialization and does not force banks to work with the best traders and trade deals due to the availability of lien on real estate.

The main risk factor in agricultural commodity trade is price risk. Many traders fail and cannot fulfill their commitments toward banks during price plunges, while traders keep hoping for an upside turn. The banks can manage such risk by a margin call, yet price volatility is a systematic risk fueled by speculation via conventional options and future contracts. Islamic restrictions provide a blueprint of a Shari'ah-compliant future contract that stabilizes market participants' prices and hinders speculation. The margin call and Islamic future contract are the subjects of this chapter. Before going into technical details of risk associated with price and addressing the issue with margin calls and future Islamic contracts,

© The Author(s), under exclusive license to Springer Nature
Switzerland AG 2023
A. S. Gundogdu, *Food Security, Affordable Housing, and Poverty*,
Palgrave Studies in Islamic Banking, Finance, and Economics,
https://doi.org/10.1007/978-3-031-27689-7_4

the following section elaborates on risk while employing Islamic trade finance contracts. Grasping the risk aspect of these contracts is key to appreciating the subject of margin calls and Islamic future contracts for the agricultural sector.

Islamic Trade Finance Contracts and Risk for Financiers

Islamic trade finance contracts can primarily be categorized into asset-based and asset-backed. In asset-backed contracts, the financier maintains ownership of the financed goods for a specific period of time. In this system, the entity seeking the loan is not perceived as a borrower but rather an obligor. This is because the contract stipulates that the responsibility of the loan seeker is to purchase the financed goods from the financier under the delivery undertaking schedule. Both asset-based and asset-backed contracts can also be categorized as import financing and export financing. The different characteristics of import and export financing would dictate varying approaches to risk management to deal with the matters related to transactions under each (Fig. 4.1).

Regarding asset-based export financing, it is a requirement that the financier should assess the off-taker credit risk in another country. In relation to asset-backed financing, the primary risk is linked to the third parties involved and the goods financed. The following sections provide details relating to the cases of each.

Risk in Asset-Based Islamic Trade Finance Contracts

For *Murabaha* import financing contracts, the leading risk linked with the contract is the credit risk of the borrower. This is because such structures are designed so that the financier will not be involved in the goods apart from providing the funds to purchase them after the shipping documents have been presented.[1] On this basis, managing risk should focus on the loan seeker that becomes borrower. Undoubtedly, the risk assessment in Islamic finance does not have to differ from conventional financing. Many studies have focused on the assessment of credit risk in conventional

---

[1] For transaction flow, refer to: Gundogdu, A. S. (2009). 2-Step Murabaha as an alternative resource mobilization tool for Islamic Banks in the context of international trade. *International Journal of Monetary Economics and Finance*, 2(3/4), 286–301.

4 FINANCING THE TRADE OF AGRICULTURAL COMMODITIES

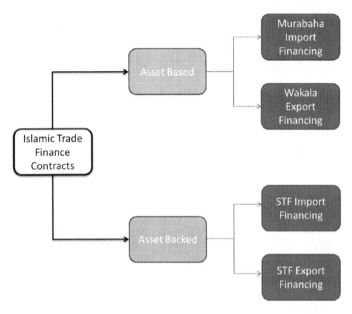

Fig. 4.1 Islamic trade finance contracts categorized (*Source* Gundogdu [2016a])

financing. Some of these studies focusing on the Asian financial crisis have concluded that there are major flaws connected with conventional finance, which annuls measures put in place to manage risk. This flaw is related to the fact that the financier cannot control how the borrower uses the funds in the course of their business once the funds have been disbursed (Gundogdu, 2014). This is an important observation because granted loans should be used in the borrower's business, where they generate the profit that will make it possible to pay back the loan. In instances where these funds are used in speculation, such as in real estate undertakings, such funds will lead to market distortion and result in problems related to non-performing loans, which often end up being the responsibility of the public through state bailouts. In its simplest form, credit risk management needs to cover the assessment of external factors like local regulations, global prices of commodities or FX, and the macroeconomic environment prevailing in different countries. It involves corporate governance and management's ability to deal with any risk emanating from these external factors and their impact on the capacity to generate cash that will enable a company to honor its obligations.

As can be seen in Fig. 4.2, for the financier, efforts to manage risk should focus on assessing external factors, scenarios for potential changes in such factors, the company managements capability to deal with changes and external factors, the impact of such factors and the changes in the company's ability to generate cash flow. In asset-based Murabaha, the profit generated by the financier is linked to the difference between the purchase and selling prices. While the selling price is the amount paid to the supplier, the concept of the sale price denotes the deferred amount to be paid by the loan seeker/borrower. For the financier, the most important consideration is the state of the borrower's future cash flow, which will determine the ability to pay the sale price. Therefore, the basis of financial analysis should be the outside forces that may impact the future generation of cash by the loan seeker, as they have a huge impact on profitability, equity and debt rations, and the asset conversion cycle.

It is possible to convert many conventional financial contracts into Shari'ah-compliant versions, especially when looking at asset-based Murabaha. Even though Islamic finance and conventional finance contracts assess risk similarly, the former has some significant merits. For instance, Islamic finance differs from conventional finance in that institutions operating in keeping with it would make disbursements against

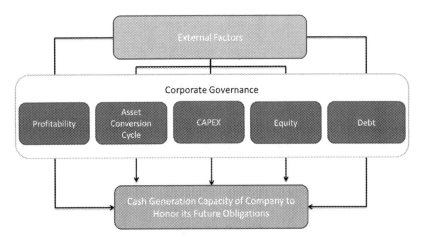

Fig. 4.2 Risk in asset-based *Murabaha* (*Source* Gundogdu [2016a])

Table 4.1 Risk management in Islamic asset-based import financing

Risk	Likely causes	Mitigants
Credit Risk of the importer in the same country	Market conditions impede the generation of enough cash at the date of maturity	Credit analysis
Debt subordination	Other lenders have a higher rank	*Pari-Passu* Clause

Source Gundogdu (2016a)

the transaction, which means they have a better understanding of what the loan will be used for. This differs from conventional finance, where the loan seeker can do whatever they want with the funds once they are disbursed to the loan seeker's account. Islamic finance keeps track of what the money is used for by paying directly to the supplier's account. This not only ensures that the loan is used in the borrower's core business but also helps financiers better understand the borrower's business. This enhanced knowledge boosts credit assessment efforts illustrated for asset-based *Murabaha* import financing in Table 4.1.

The experience gained in conventional credit analysis and its principles can also be implemented in Islamic lending. The Islamic finance industry's taking advantage of conventional finance systems would not compromise Shari'ah compliance since it only involves issues related to whether the individual seeking the loan is creditworthy and not the way the lending transaction is structured. On the other hand, there is no guarantee that rigorous credit analysis would ensure the timely repayment of loans, which is a more important factor in Islamic finance than in conventional finance. Conventional finance differs from Islamic finance in that in the former; the financiers can tolerate late payment because it means that the borrower will pay late payment fees.

The basis of Islamic asset-based Murabaha import financing contracts is not the calculation of interest. In the Shari'ah-compliant arrangement, the loan seeker is informed of the cost of financing on the disbursement date. This is also the date when the sale price is clarified. After disbursement, none of these details can be changed. For this reason, the financier incurs losses if there are delays in paying back the money. Consequently, Islamic FIs should perform more rigorous risk management. This can be done by requesting guarantees, or *Pari-Passu* clauses in the *Murabaha* contract. However, debate exists regarding potential controversies in Pari-Passu

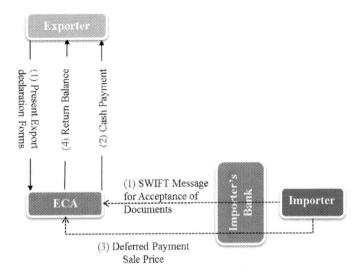

Fig. 4.3 Transaction flow for asset-based Islamic export financing (*Source* Gundogdu [2016b])

and subordination from a legal point of view. Structural subordination is where the financier was not paid on the date they were supposed to be because the company needed to pay other higher-ranking obligations like taxes and employee salaries (Caminal, 2009). If such subordination is likely, Islamic FIs can request other assurances and embed Pari-Passu clauses into the financing agreement to protect themselves from debt subordination vis-à-vis other financiers.[2]

Compared to supplier financing Wakala contracts for export financing, asset-based Murabaha contracts are easier to manage. Under the Islamic export financing schemes, Islamic FIs must shoulder the risk of off-taker from another country. Figure 4.3 illustrates the structure of asset-based export financing.

---

[2] *Pari-Passu* as explained by Investopedia: "A Latin phrase meaning 'equal footing' that describes situations where two or more assets, securities, creditors or obligations are equally managed without any display of preference. An example of pari-passu occurs during bankruptcy proceedings when a verdict is reached, all creditors can be regarded equally, and will be repaid at the same time and at the same fractional amount as all other creditors. Treating all parties the same means they are pari-passu."

Table 4.2 Risk management in Islamic asset-based export financing

Risk	Likely causes	Mitigants	Contingency
Credit risk of off-taker in another country	Market conditions impede the generation of adequate cash at the date of maturity	Credit analysis	Export receivable insurance
Debt subordination	Other lenders have a higher rank	*Pari-Passu* clause	Export receivable insurance

Source Gundogdu (2016a)

The asset-based Murabaha export risk management illustrated in Table 4.2 is intricate. For instance, it can be a massive challenge for risk management when the risk that needs to be shouldered is in another country. In certain jurisdictions, foreign entities have no permission to establish legal mortgages. In such cases, a bank guarantee would require an exposure limit setting. Even with *Pari-Passu* for the rank of debt, local lenders would devise methods of subordinating exporter's debt.

Only one viable method for mitigating debt subordination exists when a bank guarantee cannot be obtained: approaching a Takaful company to buy an export receivable insurance policy. However, there is a challenge with this type of insurance in that, in most cases, it only ensures 90% of the export value. This is done to ensure that financiers are more diligent when assessing the credit risk of the off-taker. For this reason, for proper management of risk to operate asset-based finance contracts, Islamic FIs must develop robust credit analysis capabilities. In this regard, Islamic FIs should not hesitate to take advantage of the experience gained in the conventional finance sector.

Risk in Asset-Backed Islamic Trade Finance Contracts

Asset-backed Murabaha contracts require that the financier owns the purchased goods. Such contracts are entered into to operate structured trade finance facilities. The basis of such structures is that the financier will purchase commodities considered easy to market as requested by the loan seeker/obligor. Such commodities are then stored in a warehouse—in most cases bonded—close to where the loan seeker is located and only release ownership of the commodities once the payment from the loan seeker/obligor has been received. These kinds of structures are cash and carry arrangements and collateral assumed in the form of financed commodities as opposed to traditional collateral like mortgages. The case of Black Sea wheat import financing illustrating this point is presented in Fig. 4.4. Following the acceptance of the offer signed between the Islamic FI and the loan seeker/obligor based on the Murabaha agreement, the following steps occur:

  i. The beneficiary pays a deposit of between 20 and 30% of the invoice value to the Islamic FI on the date of the financing request, based on the price volatility of that day.
 ii. The goods are shipped, and documents are presented.
iii. One hundred percent of the invoice amount is paid to the supplier by the Islamic FI.
 iv. Once the local agent bank receives the documents, it is instructed by the Islamic FI to deliver them to the collateral management (CM).

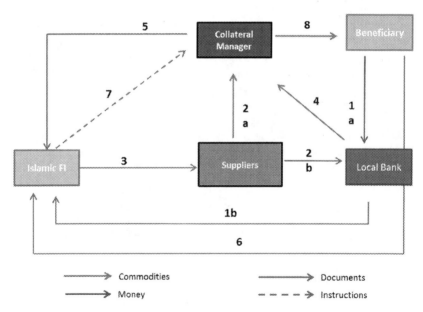

Fig. 4.4 Transaction scheme of asset-backed *Murabaha* (*Source* Gundogdu [2016a])

v. CM facilitates the delivery of the commodities to the bonded warehouse. The warehouse receipt is issued to the Islamic FI for its commodities.
vi. The beneficiary makes the payment for the value of commodities it needs to the Islamic FI through the local agent bank.
vii. Once payment has been received, the Islamic FI instructs the CM to release the goods.

If the obligor (the loan seeker) cannot clear the goods within a specific period, the financier can defray their expenses by selling them to other off-takers. In a typical Murabaha trade finance facility, some involved third parties include the off-takers, facility agents, insurance companies, and collateral managers. Typically, the local bank plays the role of the facility agent and manages the day-to-day disbursement-repayment transaction on the ground. The off-takers are the third parties under obligation based on the purchase contract to purchase goods made available based on agreed specifications.

Asset-backed Murabaha contracts could be in the form of an export financing facility against the assignment of sales contracts and export receivables. Regarding export financing, the major purpose of risk management is to employ export receivables for mitigating FX and credit risks. Regarding asset-backed export financing, the leading difference from asset-based financing is the risk linked to off-takers in export markets (Gundogdu, 2014). Asset-backed *Murabaha* differs from asset-based Murabaha in that the loan seeker is not perceived as a borrower. Still, an obligor and third parties with certain responsibilities exist to mitigate the lender's risk.

Consequently, as indicated in Fig. 4.5, the risk categories differ compared to those of asset-based Murabaha. The suggested techniques for managing risk in asset-backed Murabaha are meant to make available a framework for conducting structured financing solutions for Islamic FI interacting with international traders. Based on this framework, Islamic FIs can design fitting financial structures based on the distinctive needs of their clients based on the transaction and commodity financed. The suggested framework not only provides trade finance solutions but also focuses on building and marketing suitable novel credit enhancement and risk management solutions that can lure funds and banks to channel liquidity/resources to asset-backed *Murabaha* transactions. The next section elaborates on the risk aspect in asset-backed Murabaha transactions, namely performance risk, collateral risk, and legal risk.

Performance Risk

This class of risk is linked to the primary entities participating in the transaction cycle and the potential causes and impact if their intervention is not performed adequately. Some risks may be attributed to fraud, negligence, errors, mistakes, or lack of competence. Some involved parties include collection account banks, freight forwarders, insurance underwriters, shipping companies, transporters, off-takers, collateral managers, and beneficiaries.

Regarding the obligor, performance risk is related to attitude and capability to produce or sell goods notwithstanding the circumstances like uncertainty on the political front. The risk is also linked to the overall external environment influencing the ability of the beneficiary to honor its obligation, especially about purchasing the commodities based on the purchase undertaking schedule below:

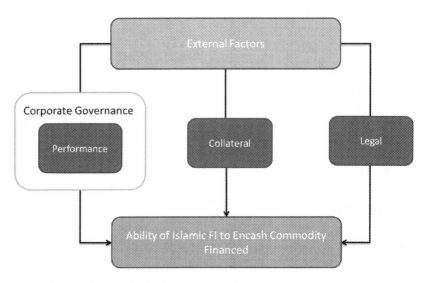

Fig. 4.5 Risk in asset-backed *Murabaha* (*Source* Gundogdu [2016a])

- Presence of import duty in the export market and quota or license in the domestic market. It is vital to check (if they exist) on an ongoing basis.
- Beneficiary's risk management characteristics, including commodity price risk and FX risk.

It is the financier's responsibility to evaluate whether the beneficiary can deal with any risk flowing from the above areas. This can be checked by assessing the beneficiary's corporate governance standards to determine whether the beneficiary has adequate systems to deal with the potential risks. As part of due diligence, representatives of the financier should pay physical visits to the producer. Among these representatives should be third-party experts who can accurately evaluate the entity's capability to deal with any envisaged challenges. Table 4.3 presents some aspects that a team conducting due diligence needs to focus on.

The obligor should also supply the following documents:

- Bylaws/memo/articles of association
- Board of directors, members, and position
- List of senior staff/management backgrounds or experience and references/structure diagram
- List of shareholders with equity distribution
- Last three years audited financial statements (if applicable)
- The purchase/sale contracts (sample when and where required)
- The import/export license (if any and where applicable)

Table 4.3 Eligibility criteria for the obligor

Beneficiary	The obligor should have a proven operational track record (ability to produce or process)
	The obligor should have a solid business track record (ability to export or sell locally)
	The obligor should be reputable and has previous experience in the particular business to be financed
	The obligor should not have pending dispute or investigation for fraud or similar (to be rejected if recurrent)
	Existence of quotas, import/export licenses, tariff barriers, VAT, and other mandatory regulations

Source Gundogdu (2016a)

- Understanding/commitment letters of the pre-approved off-takers
- Contracts and export receivables assignment agreements
- Transactions volumes per commodity for the last three years
- List of major customers for the last three years
- Relevant current financials, technical and operational information evidencing the obligor's ability to operate, produce process, and sell successfully.

Considering how the financing of cross-border physical commodities works, it can be challenging to envisage how asset-backed Murabaha's risk can be assessed without the participation of well-insured, capable, and professional third parties managing collateral. For this reason, robust eligibility criteria, especially the presence of suitable professional indemnity insurance, must be observed in selecting and building relationships with the collateral manager, as illustrated in Table 4.4.

Apart from the collateral manager and loan seeker/obligor, some third parties' collateral risk should also be considered. For instance, the freight forwarder's performance capability and the insurance underwriter's integrity should also be assessed. Some aspects that can be considered in this case include a review of membership with international bodies like the International Federation of Freight Forwarders

Table 4.4 Eligibility criteria/responsibility for the collateral manager

Collateral manager	CM must be independent and of repute with a proven experience in the relevant fields (the country and the type of commodity)
	CM may be rated by an international rating agency of an investment grade
	The collateral manager must provide acceptable **professional indemnity insurance** to cover errors, omissions, fraud and collusions, and willful conduct from reputable insurers
	CM agreement to clearly define the role of each party with clear responsibilities of each contracting party
	CM agreement to ensure full control of the commodity by CM at all times with the title of the commodity to the financier
	Monitoring reports are regularly received from the CM

Source Gundogdu (2016a)

Associations (FIATA). Regarding the off-takers, the criteria below can be helpful:

- Off-takers (the obligor's customers) need to have a proven willingness to honor contractual agreements, be strong economically, have good creditworthiness, and be financially sound. Where they exist, pre-signed sales contracts with off-takers should be requested. In some instances, there may be a need to do a credit assessment.
- The obligor of the structured trade finance (loan-seeking trader) should advise the off-takers of the notice of assignments. When this has occurred, the off-takers should acknowledge and irretrievably promise to pay for the dues receivables of the assigned contract in the assigned collection account. The message used to do the assignment can be like the one in Table 4.5.

- For export financing, letters of credit confirmed/issued by the bank acceptable to the Islamic FI must be preferred.
- Once an off-taker gains a reputation, an open account, and a proven track record, documentary collection may be acceptable against export receivable insurance coverage.

Shipment, transporting, processing, and storage pose a risk in asset-backed Murabaha. Risks may be related to moving the commodity, whether processed or raw, to the markets where it will be sold and payment received. Mainly, the process relates to risks and challenges linked with collateral management and warehousing. Some of the challenges and applicable mitigants include:

- Implementing financing in tranches connected to the inventory build-up scheduled in case of tolling arrangements. It also involves getting the usage of goods to align with the repayment schedules. This makes it possible to supervise raw materials and finished commodities' release appropriately.
- Special care needs to be taken for perishable and non-perishable products, especially regarding storage conditions, production, and delivery schedules. This is why there is a need to ensure that conditions in warehouses are suitable for specific commodities.

Table 4.5 Assignment of receivable

We hereby inform you that in the context of financing agreement No: XX dated XX/XX/XXX, concluded with the financier, the contract proceeds were assigned to the financier. Therefore, you are kindly requested to irrevocably commit to paying any amount pertaining to the contract to the following account of the financier:

Account Name:
A/C No:
Bank Name:
SWIFT Code:

The Contract No: XXXX

Please sign and stamp below for your confirmation end send it to the financier.

We hereby acknowledge and confirm to pay the proceeds of the contract mentioned above into the financier account.
Name:
Signature:
Stamp:

Source Gundogdu (2016a)

- For both the financier and the CM, it is vital to apply a dependable system for monitoring.
- In some countries, when the warehousing holder or the collateral manager is not appropriately licensed, significant risks may exist, particularly if such countries have not been implementing warehousing for a long time.
- Identifying an independent and internationally reputable warehouse operator.
- Independent professionals should inspect the collateral on an ongoing basis and be marked to show any deterioration in grade and quality by the time it gets to market.
- Monitor whether collateral may have caused environmental degradation, such as when oil products stored in tanks contaminate the environment.

The above issues make it necessary to pay attention when selecting a warehousing facility and collateral manager. The eligibility criteria for the collateral manager have been presented above. With regard to the warehousing facility, the following eligibility criteria should be observed:

- Location, security, and ability to satisfy local health and safety regulations should be the primary considerations when identifying a warehousing facility.
- The warehousing facility should be independent, and the legal owner should only be a custodian of the goods they have been requested to store. This implies that the warehouse operator should not have any ownership interest in the goods they keep.
- It is acceptable to have a field warehouse as long as there is an independent and qualified CM to take exclusive and total control of the goods stored in it. There should be signs around the warehouse to indicate this.
- None of the third parties, including the insurance company, inspection company, CM, and the entity that provided the funds to construct the warehouse, should have any substantial lien on the goods stored in the warehouse while they are still in storage, and the financier has not received repayment.

- A multi-peril insurance cover should exist for the warehouse to cover landslides, collapse, crumbling, theft, typhoons, flooding, and fire, among other such calamities.

Collateral Risks

Collateral risks are linked to collateral in margins, legal aspects, and commodity knowledge. Regarding collateral, the risk analysis could be linked to the aspects that follow:

- Title of the property (control and ownership)
- Rights enforceability (legal titled)
- Risk of misappropriation
- General liability during standard storage (third-party liability associated with the collateral, including the risk of damage to assets of others)
- Market value
- Experience and ability of the CM in the area of the commodity
- Liquidity/disposable (being able to liquidate collateral where need be).

From a legal standpoint, the financier needs to be able to guarantee the enforceability of the warehouse receipt as evidence of ownership in the country of the entity operating the warehouse. Thus, the main mitigant for this type of risk relies on the legal view of an independent legal course. Regarding margins, any drop in commodity price, the collateral, can wear away the consistency and correlation between the financier's exposure and the collateral's value. Many case studies related risk management measures for dealing with such erosion (Claessens & Duncan, 1993). Nonetheless, standard financial techniques of hedging are usually not Shari'ah compliant. To deal with this risk, Islamic FIs use cash deposits.

The following section will present a methodology for computing the cash deposit margin to manage the margin. The collateral's financing value should not be more than the current fair market value of the collateral at the time of the disbursement. As soon as possible, commodity collateral should be mark-to-market if there exists any signs of material depreciation in value (no matter the reason) or lack of performance by the obligor. Furthermore, in such circumstances, it is necessary to revalue the commodity collateral, and a professional appraiser must conduct this job, and such efforts should avoid overreliance on quantitative techniques. The underlying financing agreement must fully reflect the procedure. To avert embezzlement, willful misconduct, and third-party liability of collateral manager, marine insurance and professional indemnity insurance should be available. The CM should be chosen based on their experience managing the subject commodity in the country. Also, to avert challenges if the collateral is liquidated, where the obligor is unable to purchase the commodity, criteria for eligible commodity should be in place (Gundogdu, 2014):

- The commodity must be subject to perishability under standard storage conditions over a reasonable period.
- It is safe and easy to handle the commodity and is not subject to hazardous implications or dangerous manipulation.
- The commodity can be easily marketed.
- Standby-off-takers exist because the commodity market is liquid.
- The commodity is fungible.
- The commodity is at the mid-stream of the downstream level.
- Supply and demand dynamics determine the price of the commodity within the market.
- The commodity is listed and traded in the applicable future markets such as LIFEE, ICE, or the CME group.
- Regarding transactions involving imports of the commodity's technical specifications, quantity, and quality, independent and globally accredited surveyors of inspection companies should analyze the product at the port where it is loaded and, if need be, at the port where it is unloaded or in the storage facilities.
- The character of the commodity and the transition's life cycle should be linked, and the former should never go beyond the commodity's life duration.
- There should be appropriate hedging of the goods and proceeds where applicable and required.

Legal Risks

Notwithstanding all the diligence, some significant issues may remain. For this reason, there is a need for a robust legal department to measure, manage, and monitor the changing legal frameworks in the markets of subjects:

- When drafting the financing and other related agreements, special care must be taken, considering the overriding norm of local statutes on pledges and security.
- Legal views on local laws in all applicable documentation and jurisdictions relating to the security of interests.
- Transferability/negotiability issues: Negotiable Warehouse Receipt Act not framed (or not yet sufficient).
- The bank's claims as a secured owner or creditor must be high in rank and be made legally perfect, as shown by legal views and existing procedures for quick realization of the collateral.
- To keep other creditors at bay, the financier must clearly label the collateral with markings showing ownership or pledge.
- Considering the need to mark-to-market the commodity collateral and it is possible to call the margins if necessary, it is vital to reflect these features in the underlying financing agreement fully.
- A competent and independent legal counsel is employed.
- Negative pledge clauses to ensure that no assignment, transfer, or sale generates any added security interest under the use of shipments or goods (if needed).
- Legal documentation at the beneficiary level (registration certificate, by-laws, articles of association) and the country level (title of property, FX).

There is a need to ensure the legal enforceability of the physical collateral or receivables. If any security is assumed over the commodity collateral, a legal point of view should be obtained endorsing enforceability and precedence over all pertinent statutes. Moreover, security interests must be timely and appropriately perfected. It is vital to ensure that the legal contrivances relating to the pledging of receivables, sold or assigned, are robust and that the financier's rights over the proceeds are clear. There should also be efforts to observe all local steps related to secure registration, and the financier needs to obtain a legal point of view on applicable jurisdictions. The fundamental agreement and existing legal remedies need to enable the financier to liquidate the collateral or proceed without wasting too much time after default and be able to sell and collect receivables.

Based on the above insights, it can be noted that the transaction is properly framed, and the risk is fundamentally externalized to the CM from the obligor. The CM is perceived to be a reliable third party that makes available an indemnity insurance policy stipulating that the financier is a loss payee. If you consider that the structure heavily depends on the financed goods ownership and third parties like the CM, it is vital to ensure that proper structures are in place, such as the existence of a proper insurance policy and CM. This will ensure that risk management is managed securely.

Regarding the insurance issue, there should be clear criteria for eligibility, such as:

i. There should be adequate insurance for the commodity at every stage against deterioration or loss during transportation, unloading, and storage.
ii. A reliable and sound insurance company must be used to underwrite land and marine insurance, and the goods should be reinsured by an international re-insurance company that's investment rated.
iii. In all the insurance policies, the financier must be the loss payee.
iv. Procedures for claim and recovery must be defined clearly and adequately documented.

Relating to insurance policy commodities, loss payee clauses could introduce loopholes into the system. Considering that insurance service providers, including Takaful, will refuse to honor a claim if the premium for a specified period has not been paid or the entity that the policy insures is insolvent. In relation to this, Islamic FIs need to monitor not just the financial health of entities but also the payment of insurance premiums when making decisions concerning Murabaha deals. The preferred method of dealing with insurance risk is to be directly assured of the insurance policy. This implies that Islamic financiers can manage risk better if a policy is purchased for each asset-backed Murabaha contract.

Focusing on means of managing the primary issues regarding risk management and providing a profitable and safe financing environment for both the loan seekers/obligors and financiers in asset-backed Murabaha deals ends here. Managing performance risk, collateral risk, and legal risk necessitates strong institutional capacity. This is the main challenge to bringing more Islamic FIs to the structured agricultural trade finance. The presence of Licensed Warehouses (LWs) with national regulations can address these risk aspects and provide a platform for Islamic FIs to channel more funds for the sector. The Licensed Warehouse is expected to be a pillar of agricultural finance with embedded features of standard and conformity assessment labs attached to their facilities and electronic Warehouse Receipts (e-WR). E-WRs can be used to develop Shari'ah-compliant Islamic Future contracts to enhance price stability for both farmers and agricultural processors.

In asset-based Murabaha contracts, the risk aspect shares, unlike asset-backed Murabaha, similarities with conventional finance contracts. It can be posited that the asset-based Murabaha is better because it involves disbursing funds into suppliers' accounts, making it easier to determine what the funds are used for. Nonetheless, practices involved in managing risk by conventional financing can, to an extent, be modified to fit the bill. On the other hand, the management of risk for asset-based Murabaha calls for the establishment of appropriate techniques for dealing with risks unique to Islamic FIs. Under asset-backed Murabaha financing, the ownership aspect makes it impossible to make a claim that could arise from the obligor's debt subordination and debt to other creditors. Yet, possession of ownership also leads to other risks, as alluded to earlier. It is known to all professionals involved in finance that all deals involve a certain level of risk. Thus, the main issue is not related to the total elimination of risk but finding ways of dealing with it. Following an assessment and identification of risks, it can be:

- Transferred via ECA coverage, transport insurance, of storage insurance, among others.
- Mitigated through measures like offshore collection, employing a collateral manager, fixed price contracts, hard currency off-takers, offshore receivables, or heading.
- Shared via such means as the involvement of other financiers, ECA coverage, or deposit margin.
- Managed using robust procedures, monitoring, controls, and supervision.
- Taken using force majeure where no other alternative exists, even though this method is seldom employed.

Undoubtedly, Islamic finance principles may require finance providers to assume risk and lean in the direction of asset-backed Murabaha. The more closely financiers want to follow the dictates of Islamic finance, the more they will want to use asset-backed Murabaha. Asset-backed Murabaha differs from asset-based Murabaha in that the successful implementation of the former requires third parties to be involved. Third parties include the Takaful/insurance providers, warehouse operators, and CM. It is not just expected but also crucial for the Islamic finance sector to establish a relationship with these parties, especially the Takaful providers, to properly deal with the risk connected to the ownership of financed goods under an asset-backed Murabaha contract. The next section delves into price risk management in Islamic assets back in Murabaha with Margin calls. Since commodities are the main collateral, sharp price drops can lead to collateral impairment. Hence, a systematic way of price monitoring and margin call management is needed to ensure the healthy practice of asset-backed Murabaha.

MARGIN CALL

Murabaha Sale: Asset-Based or Asset-Backed

As briefly described in the previous section, because the Islamic FIs do not return ownership but transfer it to the borrower that is willing to commit to a fixed return repayment, asset-based Murabaha is seen by certain critics as having the following weaknesses:

Debt creation: Regarding an asset-based Murabaha sale, ownership transfer from the supplier to the financier and from the financier to the loan seeker occurs simultaneously. To determine whether the transaction is genuine, the invoice of shipping documents should be presented. However, some scholars highlight that Islamic finance needs to be based on principles involving sharing profit and risk. Hence, it is argued that the creation of debt obligation in asset-based Murabaha should produce the same result as conventional finance (Yousef, 2004).

Markup: Relating to asset-based Murabaha, the loan seeker makes their request known using a form of offer, asking the lender to purchase specific goods and making a commitment that they will purchase the said goods from the lender with a pre-determined markup. Based on a form of acceptance, the lender makes the commitment to involve in the transaction. Late payment charges are another aspect of markup. It is not permissible in Islamic FIs to charge any added markup after the maturity date if the borrower's payments are delayed. Nonetheless, there have been cases of Islamic banks imposing such charges, blurring the difference between Islamic and conventional finance.

Collateral: In the same way conventional finance institutions would, Islamic institutions typically require collateral of different forms, including guarantees and mortgages. This ensures that the Murabaha-created debt is paid back as per schedule. This has also led to criticism.

Risk and agency: In a similar manner as conventional banks, Islamic banks work hard to avoid quality-related challenges. When designing asset-based Murabaha contracts, the main aim is to appoint the loan seeker as a bank's undisclosed agent to deal with insurance processes, quality control, and purchase contract. Under the Murabaha contract, the loan seeker agrees that they will buy the goods from the financier as they are. This arrangement would essentially transfer all risks linked with the transaction to the loan seeker.

Even though a Murabaha sale complies with Shari'ah, the criticism above should not be dismissed offhand. Some of the noted weaknesses can be addressed through asset-backed Murabaha to a certain degree. In summary, it can be noted that asset-backed Murabaha is cash and carry financing, where the financier owns the purchased goods while in storage until the sale to the loan seeker has been accomplished. This is comparable to the conventional bank's commodity pledge. However, the system in asset-backed Murabaha differs from pledge commodity in that direct ownership by the financier is a requirement in the former. The flow of transactions in the asset-backed Murabaha is illustrated in Fig. 4.6. The illustration uses the case of a sugar refinery, which promises to buy the sugar brought to the warehouse by the financier.

i. The sugar refinery pays 15% of the invoice amount into the financier's account.
ii. The shipping documents are made available after the shipment of the sugar.
iii. The financier pays the raw sugar supplier.
iv. The raw sugar is delivered to the sugar refinery warehouse under collateral management, and the CM provides the financier with a warehouse receipt.
v. Once the sugar refinery requests that the raw sugar be released, the financier sends an instruction to the CM to take custody of

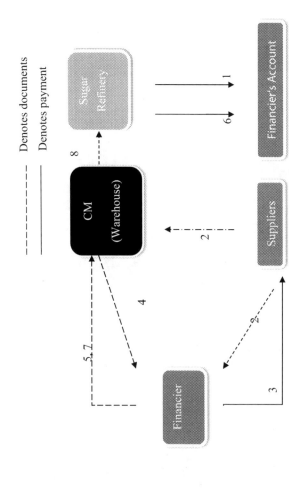

Fig. 4.6 Schematic flow of the transaction (*Source* Gundogdu [2014])

the refined white sugar (based on the conversion factor of 93%). Once the financier has taken custody of the refined sugar, they instruct that the raw sugar be released for refining.

vi. The sugar refinery sends a request for refined white sugar and makes a payment into the financier's account.

vii. The CM receives an instruction from the financier to release the refined sugar as payment would have been received.

viii. The sugar refinery receives refined sugar.

When the financier gets the documents for payment, the financier will take measures to ensure that the funds amounting to 15% of the invoice amount are reflected in their account. The financier has the leverage to increase the deposit margin to 25%, where they believe it is necessary based on price forecasts and market conditions. The financier will also ensure that the 85% to be funded will deliver a minimum of 117% against the prevailing prices before any disbursement. The financier will then instruct that the documents are sent to the CM, who anticipates the shipment's delivery. The CM ensures the safe transportation of goods from the port to the warehouse, where it is verified that they are as supposed to be. When the CM takes custody of the goods, the CM issues a warehouse receipt in the financier's name.

At the time the sugar refinery needs to start refining the raw sugar, they send a request that the financier releases the sugar. The financier sends a request to the CM, asking them to take custody of an equal amount of refined sugar before any raw sugar is released for refining. The refined sugar remains under the custodianship of the CM until the sugar refinery requests it. At this point, an invoice is made by the financier to the sugar refinery relating to the requested quantities with the associated management fees and markup. The sugar refinery will receive a copy of the invoice and the release instruction after paying the invoice amount.

Asset-backed Murabaha differs from asset-based Murabaha in that the former requires a specific degree of knowledge regarding the commodity for which the finance is being made available. This is related to the fact that ownership will remain with the financier to constitute collateral. The details that need to be known include the type of commodity, local and global regulation and quotas, price indexes, significant exporters and importers, and production and consumption figures. Possession of ownership of the commodity during the transaction exposes the financier to certain risks, which calls for sound management of risk.

Commodity Price Risk Management

Regarding whether trade finance facilities succeed or fail, asset-backed Murabaha structures can be grouped in terms of proper identification and management of risk (MacNamara, 2008). In the structure alluded to above, four risk areas exist: commodity, third party, company, and country-related risk. Islamic FIs differ from conventional financial institutions in that the former does not have the advantage of using the most available hedging methods because they have to adhere to Shari'ah law. Substantial losses are always possible because Islamic finance requires the financier to rely on ownership of the financed commodity as collateral. Another crucial aspect is collateral damage. Takaful Islamic insurance is the method employed to deal with the possible damage of collateral, including deterioration of collateral during storage, accidents, or misappropriation.

As indicated earlier, in Islamic finance, using conventional derivative instruments for hedging against commodity price risk is not an option. This is because these derivative instruments like options, futures, or forward do not comply with Shari'ah. More importantly, they give rise to price volatility, increasing the risk in agricultural commodity trade financing. Establishing protocols and methods for managing risk related to commodity prices is most required when proposing asset-backed Murabaha as an alternative. The financier depends on the loan seeker's cash deposit, as seen in Fig. 4.6. Typically, there is an increase in the cash deposit from 15 to 25%, depending on the personal judgment concerning the price volatility of the financed agricultural commodity. If the price appears volatile, the cash deposit required is also higher. Nonetheless, no established scientific method exists when computing the cash deposit margin, security margin for financiers. It is not just the commodity that determines the cash deposit to be charged but also the tenor of financing. This is because tenor may introduce higher price volatility. This is illustrated by Fig. 4.7, which presents the last 30 years of sugar prices.

From an analysis of Fig. 4.7, a pattern becomes clear, but the cash deposit percentage requested for sugar financing under asset-backed Murabaha requires further data processing. The next section elaborates on a method for security margin calculation and managing commodity price risk with margin call procedures.

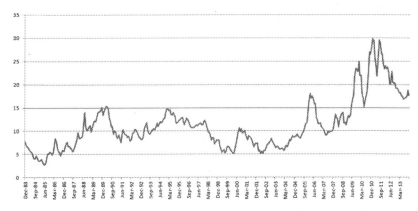

Fig. 4.7 Sugar price volatility (*Source* Gundogdu [2014])

Security Margin Calculation and Margin Call
If we consider single-month descriptive statistics reflecting the change in the 30 years before 2013, as presented in Table 4.6, the average increase in the price of sugar was 0.6% with a standard deviation of 8.7% and a minimum observation of −22.3%. A deviation of 8.7% from the average would deliver a risk-managed security coverage ratio of −8.1% even though sugar prices dropped by 22.3% in a tenor of one month in the worst months.

Is 8.1% of the cash deposit requested for one month tenor for asset-backed Murabaha enough? The answer to this question is a yes. Supposedly the deposit was 15%, as presented in Fig. 4.6, the security

Table 4.6 Descriptive Statistics for one-month sugar price change

Mean	0.006039
Standard error	0.004609
Standard deviation	0.087322
Sample variance	0.007625
Kurtosis	1.144287
Range	0.6035
Minimum	−0.223
Maximum	0.3805
Sum	2.1681
Count	359

Source Gundogdu (2014)

coverage ratio is 117.64%. To illustrate this point, let's imagine that the financier holds a pound of sugar valued at $1 and only paid $0.85 to assume such collateral. In that case, we can say that the sugar costs the financier $0.85 per pound; the price in the market is $1 per pound. If any reduction consumes up to a $0.15 cash deposit, the price will have to be reduced by 17.64%. Therefore, to attain security coverage of 8.1% as computed from the mean and standard deviation, the financier should ask for a cash deposit of 7.5% (8.1% = 7.5%/(100%−7.5%)).

Cash deposit would be calculated from the security coverage ratio as indicated in Eq. 4.1:

$$\text{Cash deposit} = \frac{(100 \times \text{Security Coverage Ratio})}{(100 + 100 \times \text{security coverage ratio})} \quad (4.1)$$

The security coverage ratio required for managing risk would change depending on the tenor. Longer tenors will require higher deposits. The descriptive statistics, cash deposit, and security coverage for three months, six months, and nine months tenors are presented in Table 4.7. To calculate the security coverage, the deviation is subtracted from the mean.

Notwithstanding the reality that standard deviation is suggested as the pivot when calculating, margins are only considered for downward trends and not escalations in price; the rank and percentile approach could produce a different indication. For instance, in Fig. 4.8, interest can be observed on the left side of the 0% because any escalation in the price of sugar will result in a corresponding increase in the security coverage ratio and is therefore not subject to risk management surveillance. The percentile and rank for six months tenor are presented in Fig. 4.9. The security coverage margin is computed as 21.81% based on standard deviation. Using percentile and rank, security coverage would be computed as 28.66% in a five percent confidence interval. Rank and percentile represent a more conservative approach without prejudicing the merit of standard deviation.

Already, it has been noted that Islamic FIs cannot use derivative hedging contracts to cover themselves because of issues relating to Shari'ah compliance. Similarly, such institutions can't get cash deposits and depend alone on them until the loan matures. Any commodity price decrease would lead to collateral damage, putting the financier at risk. Therefore, Islamic FIs need to adopt robust risk management practices during the period of financing. This will entail daily follow-ups on security

Table 4.7 Descriptive statistics, security coverage, and cash deposit needed for 3–6–9 month's tenor financing

3 months tenor		6 months tenor		9 months tenor	
Mean	0.02318	Mean	0.047556	Mean	0.073397
Standard error	0.009758	Standard error	0.014122	Standard error	0.017636
Standard deviation	0.18438	Standard deviation	0.265695	Standard deviation	0.330408
Sample variance	0.033996	Sample Variance	0.070594	Sample variance	0.10917
Kurtosis	2.043237	Kurtosis	0.978302	Kurtosis	2.4579
Range	1.17546	Range	1.370449	Range	2.086337
Minimum	−0.33373	Minimum	−0.38914	Minimum	−0.46684
Maximum	0.841727	Maximum	0.981308	Maximum	1.619497
Sum	8.275393	Sum	16.83491	Sum	25.76241
Count	357	Count	354	Count	351
Security coverage needed	16.12%	Security coverage needed	21.81%	Security coverage needed	25.70%
Cash deposit needed	13.88%	Cash deposit needed	17.91%	Cash deposit needed	20.45%

Source Gundogdu (2014)

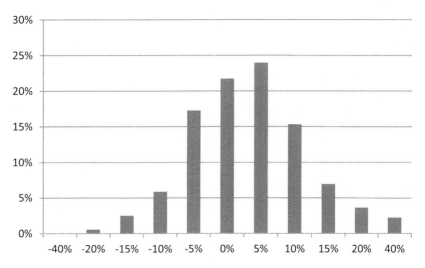

Fig. 4.8 Histogram for one-month sugar price change (*Source* Gundogdu [2014])

4 FINANCING THE TRADE OF AGRICULTURAL COMMODITIES   115

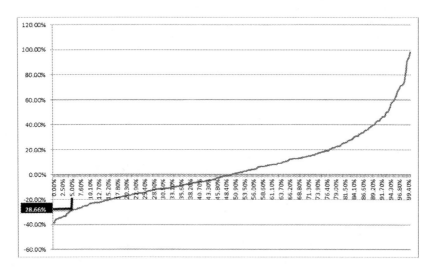

Fig. 4.9 Rank and percentile for six-month sugar price changes (*Source* Gundogdu [2014])

coverage margins and requesting that the borrower keeps the pre-agreed security coverage ratio by topping up with either the commodity or the money: margin call where need be. This complies with Islamic principles, which stipulate that the financier should take risks in exchange for the anticipated profit. However, in keeping with the character of any market participant, Islamic FIs also need to be careful when adopting risk management practices. Table 4.8 illustrates exercising margin calls for a financing tenor of six months. Margin call guidelines tend to differ by an institution and must be specifically designed based on factors like geographic region, commodity, and financing facility. For purposes of illustration, the following guidelines are assumed for calling margins in the case of the six months tenor:

  i. A 5% reduction in the price of the commodity in three days.
  ii. An 8% reduction in the price of the commodity in one month.
  iii. A 10% reduction in the price of the commodity in two months.
  iv. A 12% decrease in the price of the commodity in three months.
  v. A 14% decrease in the price of the commodity in four months.
  vi. A 16% decrease in the price of the commodity in five months.

Table 4.8 Margin Call Illustration for six-month tenor financing

Month	Price, US cents per Pound	Change in 1 month	Change in 2 month	Change in 3 month	Change in 4 month	Change in 5 month	Change in 6 month
Jan-12	24.02	2.56%	−2.04%	−8.67%	−9.83%	−16.80%	−18.49%
Feb-12	23.42	−2.50%	0.00%	−4.49%	−10.95%	−12.09%	−18.88%
Mar-12	23.79	1.58%	−0.84%	1.58%	−2.98%	−9.54%	−10.70%
Apr-12	22.48	−5.51%	−4.01%	−6.41%	−4.01%	−8.32%	−14.52%
May-12	20.27	−9.83%	−14.80%	−13.45%	−15.61%	−13.45%	−17.33%
Jun-12	20.1	−0.84%	−10.59%	−15.51%	−14.18%	−16.32%	−14.18%
Jul-12	22.76	13.23%	12.28%	1.25%	−4.33%	−2.82%	−5.25%

Source Gundogdu (2014)

On the disbursement date, in January, the price of sugar is recorded as 24.2 cents, with the commodity held until maturity in July. The recorded ending price is 22.76 cents. Suppose the commodity is held for six months, the reduction in value will only be 5.25%. Considering that the borrower paid a 17.91 deposit ahead of disbursement in January, no breach of the security coverage ratio exists. However, based on the guidelines assumed, the borrower is expected to top up in May and June. It needs to be remembered that although margins are called in May and June, the 17.91% cash deposit is enough to cover the financing period. Moreover, from a practical perspective, the loan seeker would request regular sugar release to be processed throughout the six months, with low amounts of sugar remaining in the warehouse when the six months end. This lowers the value-at-risk.

Notwithstanding that it has been subject to a great deal of criticism, asset-based Murabaha has an important role in keeping with the "FAS-2: *Murabaha* and *Murabaha* to the Purchase Order" standard developed by Accounting and Auditing Organization for Islamic Financial Institutions. Even in their simple state, Murabaha contracts connect financing have a lower risk of creating liquidity bubbles because they are usually associated with genuine economic transactions. As presented in this book, asset-backed Murabaha can also deliver considerable service, considering that Islamic FIs have experience managing risk linked with holding ownership of financed commodities during a specific tenor.

In a comparable manner to asset-based Murabaha contracts, the asset-backed type has also been criticized. If this criticism is considered, it can potentially make the Islamic finance industry healthier. The main areas of criticism are linked to cash deposits, not paid when there is a default by the loan seeker in asset-backed Murabaha. This kind of conduct can violate Islamic Shari'ah principles prohibiting contractual penalties.[3] Nonetheless, regarding day-to-day business down payment can be requested, and the amount may or may not be returned to the payer if they do not fulfill a specific promise. Even though this analogy may not be the best of Islamic Fiqh, it can be used to illustrate this point. A landlord may request a potential buyer in a real estate deal to make a down payment so that the latter does not miss an opportunity to sell to another buyer in case the former changes their mind. If this practice is

---

[3] See pp. 200. Ahmad, A. U. F. (2010). *Theory and practice of modern Islamic finance: The case analysis from Australia.* Brown Walker Press.

perceived as keeping with Shari'ah principles for individuals, what could make it a problem for businesses? It is vital that Islamic Shari'ah is to be implemented; it must be consistent for all.

The security coverage approach described above as a tool for managing risk may not wholly cover potential losses. However, it can stop the losses for the FIs involved at a certain level by monitoring the market and margin calls. Eventually, the principles of Islamic finance neither suggest return without any risk nor irresponsible taking of risk. As presented in this book, the management of price risk constitutes only a single aspect of risk management in asset-backed Murabaha. Other facets related to ensuring and maintaining beneficial ownership of commodities, which calls for wide-ranging commodity knowledge and collaborating with third parties like warehouse operators, insurance brokers, and collateral management companies. The recent development in licensed warehouses and electronic warehouse receipts provides the necessary infrastructure to mitigate such risks. Islamic banks can use this avenue for liquidity management (i.e., provide more funds for agricultural commodity trade finance). For Islamic FIs, following this course in asset-backed Murabaha calls for robust due diligence and ensuring that Islamic finance is used for genuine transactions. For this reason, Islamic FIs, as investment agents, are crucial for providing a service to account holders and channeling funds for genuine and solid transactions. The defined risk factors of performance, collateral and legal risk can be addressed by Licensed Warehousing platforms. The risk mitigated with Licensed Warehouses would allow more Islamic FIs to channel their resources to the agricultural sector.

The novelty of asset-backed Murabaha with Licensed Warehouses for agricultural commodity trading can also pave the way for Islamic future contracts. The next section explains the Islamic alternative that has emerged out of asset-backed Murabaha to conventional derivatives. Unlike conventional derivatives, Islamic future contracts can be based on real commodities owned under asset-backed Murabaha. The proposed Islamic future contract can play the role of liquidity management for Islamic banks, provide price stability for agricultural food processors, and protect smallholder farmers.

ISLAMIC FUTURE CONTRACT AND LIQUIDITY MANAGEMENT

The Islamic finance sector has enjoyed sustainable growth since its early days in the 1970s. This happened because of growing populations and increasing income from oil in OIC countries. Islamic banks became necessary as conventional finance's intricacy and product range also started increasing. They were established to ensure that those who want to follow the principles of Islam have an alternative. However, the challenges related to liquidity management for treasury functions resulted in some scholars criticizing Islamic banks. These Islamic scholars evaluated examples of some cases for the treasury function ranging from the *Maqasid Al'Ahariah* point of view, which issued temporary Fatwa until a Shari'ah-compliant alternative was found.[4]

Notwithstanding the criticism, typical Islamic finance contracts, including *Istisna*, *Ijara*, *Mudaraba*, and *Murabaha*, represent a strong possibility to serve Maqasid Al-Shari'ah equally robustly features for managing credit risk inherent in the lending process itself. Some of the criticism relating to the practices of Islamic banks lacks a rational foundation. For instance, some scholars charge that Islamic banks extensively rely on Murabaha sales (Yousef, 2004). However, this criticism usually ignores the very character of Islamic finance itself. Islamic finance can be seen as a mirror of the real economy. For instance, if nine out of ten transactions in any economy relate to trade finance, it comes as a given that nine out of ten contracts used for trade finance shall be Murabaha-based while the remainder will be subject to project finance; therefore, *Istisna* and *Ijara*. Moreover, in every attempt to scrutinize Islamic finance, it is vital to consider the profit-loss-sharing concerning less profitable and high-risk deals. Most of the controversial discussion around Islamic finance is more complicated than meets the eye. To deal with the noted problems based on a robust underpinning, the following section refers to Chapter 2 that elaborated on controversial novelty in Islamic finance. Any new program that wants to have strong Shari'ah foundations will need to avoid these.

---

[4] *Al-Maqasid Al-Shari'ah*; as per Chapra Human Development and Well-Being to be realized by ensuring the enrichment of: *Nafs* (Human self), *Mal* (Wealth), *Nasl* (Posterity), *Aql* (Intellect), and *Din* (Faith).

Shari'ah Non-compliant Products on the Stage

When evaluating any Islamic product, the process should begin with ensuring that it complies with *Maqasid Al-Shari'ah* and that the transaction being facilitated is genuine. Part of determining the genuineness of the transaction involves determining how beneficial the product will be in terms of social welfare. Commonly, a product may meet the requirements of Islamic practice but still overlook *Maqasid Al-Shari'ah*. A few examples illustrate this, such as using a Murabaha sale to buy arms of war, luring households to get over-indebted with consumption loans, and creating cash loan balloons that have no connection to the real economy. With this in mind, currently, the majority of controversial contemporary Islamic finance products like hedging tools, treasury liquidity management, and Sukuk came into being based on three kinds of novelty, as was described in Chapter 2:

 i. Bai Al-Inah
 ii. Islamic Discounting/Factoring (*Bai Al-Dayn*)
 iii. Commodity *Murabaha* based on Organized *Tawarruq*.

Shari'ah Compliant Alternatives from the Grassroots

E-Warehouse Receipt (E-WR)-based asset-backed Murabaha transactions for agricultural commodities in a licensed warehouse have great embedded features. Conventionally, operations involved asset-backed Murabaha were employed in financing commodities kept in warehouses. The financier takes the stored commodity as collateral. Unlike the asset-based Murabaha, where syndication banks and the liquidity managing bank (LMB) take the risk of RMB, in asset-backed *Murabaha*, since the ownership remains with LMB risk management, features are very different. The LMB is exposed to price volatility and risk linked to financed commodity ownership, such as insurance, quantity, and quality. In licensed warehousing, where all the physical commodities should be present against EWR for agricultural commodities, the extension of asset-backed Murabaha from a typical bonded warehouse to a licensed warehouse is possible. Considering that an electronic platform already exists for trading e-warehouse receipts, adding and signing for asset-backed Murabaha on the same platform, as indicated in Fig. 4.10, would provide banks with another liquidity management tool.

4 FINANCING THE TRADE OF AGRICULTURAL COMMODITIES   121

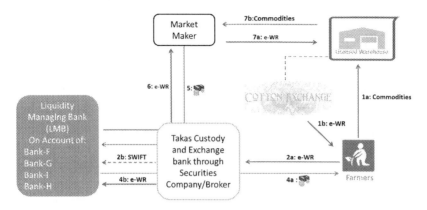

Fig. 4.10 Liquidity management based on asset-backed *Murabaha* through physical commodities in licensed warehouses (*Source* The author)

i. Farmers deliver commodities to the licensed warehouse, where the warehouse operator issues (e-WR) to these farmers through the commodity exchange.
ii. The supplier places the e-WR with a broker, then LMB receives a payment request against ownership transfer of e-WR.
iii. The minimum security merging amounting to 20% of the e-WR is paid by the market maker.
iv. The local supplier receives a payment of 100% of the invoice value from the banks through the LMB account in Takas custody and exchange bank through a broker.
v. Once the payment is validated, the broker transfers ownership of the number of commodities sold to the market maker.
vi. The market maker assumed physical delivery of the commodities.

In the transaction described above, the market maker plays a vital role because they signed the asset-backed Murabaha with the LMB. In the agreement, there are several provisions:

- The LMB will purchase an e-WR receipt once the commodities have been transferred into the licensed warehouse.
- The market maker contributes 20% cash margin.
- The farmers receive 100% payment from the LMB.

- If the price decreases, the LMB reserves the right to request a margin call to which the market maker responds by topping up the cash margin. So, the commodity fluctuation risk lies with the market maker.
- Based on three, six, and nine months maturities, the market maker takes delivery of the commodities. This is accompanied by the LMB and market maker signing the three, six, and nine months asset-backed Murabaha contract on the electronic platform.

Typically, market makers are significant users of soft commodities like flour mills. They aim to have the price fixed during harvest when wheat prices are likely to be at their lowest. This ensures that they have adequate wheat to meet their annual production plan. They must take delivery of the physical goods at maturity. If any changes occur regarding the production plan, the market maker can use the electronic platform to transfer their obligation to other traders. The ownership remains with the LMB, which can facilitate a Mudaraba or Murabaha syndication in the international market. Since they hold ownership, the syndication banks reserve the right to sell or buy any amount of e-WR on the electronic platform. Therefore, there is a liquid secondary market.

From *Maqasid Al-Shari'ah* perspective:

- Islamic FIs are essential in facilitating and financing agricultural production because they can always use their access funds. They have an opportunity to buy and sell e-WR since a 100% physical commodity exists and there is a genuine intention for delivery.
- Farmers will benefit from better prices and available liquidity since there will likely be more buyers during harvest as Islamic FIs also become buyers.
- The market maker should be a processor of the soft commodity, ready to take physical delivery. The market maker can fix the cost of raw materials and ensure that there are no unpleasant surprises in the future. Moreover, considering the commodities will be kept in a licensed warehouse, the market maker avoids the logistics related to storage. If their production plans change, they will transfer the physical delivery obligation to other traders using the electronic platform, sometimes with some losses.

In calculating the three, six, and nine months asset-backed Murabaha (Islamic Future Contract), the LMB will use the following procedure:

Future Price = Spot price + carrying cost (mark-up, licensed warehouse storage cost, storage insurance cost) + transaction cost (fees of security broker, takes custody and exchange bank and commodity exchange)

For the system to remain, sustainable, robust risk management monitoring is required. To boost the syndication market's interest in the product, the scheme's risk rating could be increased by a Takaful in the form of political risk insurance and exigency clauses covering the negligence of third parties. When Takaful exists, it increases the risk rating, which could be attractive to risk-averse funds. Participants would positively impact increasing the liquidity in the market, and farmers would enjoy the benefit of having more prospective buyers during harvest. For processors, the benefit will be lower markup when prices are calculated in the future due to increasing demand from FIs.

Regarding Islamic FIs, their funds would be placed in genuine and Shari'ah-compliant transactions against solid collateral while supporting the agricultural sector. This structure is also suitable for agricultural food processors as they have the option to fix their input prices. Islamic finance, should it be applied appropriately, would substantially contribute to the economy's stability while creating value for all the economic actors. Unlike conventional derivatives, which fuel price volatility, the Islamic future contract stabilizes the market as future prices are more predictable. It also provides a platform for banks to invest their excess funds into the real agricultural commodity sector.

References

Ahmad, A. U. F. (2010). *Theory and practice of modern Islamic finance: The case analysis from Australia.* Brown Walker Press.

Caminal, R. (2009). To rank pari passu or not to rank pari passu: That is the question in sovereign bonds after the latest episode of the Argentine saga. *Law & Business Review of the Americas,* 15(4), 745.

Claessens, S., & Duncan, R. C. (1993). *Managing commodity price risk in developing countries.* Johns Hopkins University Press.

Financial Accounting Standard No. 2 (FAS 2). (1997). *Murabaha to the Purchase Orderer.* AAOIFI.

Gundogdu, A. S. (2009). 2-Step Murabaha as an alternative resource mobilization tool for Islamic banks in the context of international trade. *International Journal of Monetary Economics and Finance, 2*(3/4), 286–301.

Gundogdu, A. S. (2014). Margin call in Islamic finance. *International Journal of Economics and Finance, 6*(8), 205–213.

Gundogdu, A. S. (2016a). Risk management in Islamic trade finance. *Boğaziçi Journal Review of Social, Economic and Administrative Studies, 30*, 59–77. https://doi.org/10.21773/boun.30.2.4

Gundogdu, A. S. (2016b). Islamic electronic trading platform on organized exchange. *Borsa Istanbul Review, 16*(4), 249–255.

Hasanin, F. (1996). *Murabaha sale in Islamic banks*. The International Institute of Islamic Thought.

IFSB, I. F. (2005). *Guiding principles of risk management for institutions (other than Insurance Institutions) offering only Islamic financial services*. IFSB.

MacNamara, J. (2008). *Structured trade and commodity finance: What can go wrong and how to avoid it*. Woodhead Publishing Limited.

The Accounting and Auditing Organization for Islamic Financial Institutions. (1997). *Financial Accounting Standard No. 2 (FAS 2) Murabaha to the Purchase Orderer*. AAOIFI.

Yousef, T. M. (2004). The Murabaha syndrome in Islamic finance: Laws, institutions and politics. In R. Wilson (Ed.), *The politics of Islamic finance* (pp. 63–80). Edinburgh University Press.

CHAPTER 5

Financing the Production of Agricultural Commodities

The Role of Cash Crops and Cooperatives in Food Security

A cooperative is "an autonomous association of persons united voluntarily to meet their common economic, social, and cultural needs and aspirations through a jointly-owned and democratically-controlled enterprise."[1] There are seven cooperative principles:

- Cooperation
- Provision of education
- Training and information
- Autonomy and independence
- Concern for the community
- Voluntary and open membership
- Democratic member control
- Member economic participation

Cooperatives are not a peculiarity of emerging economies. They emerged from developed countries in their development process (Ortmann & King, 2007). In essence, user control, user ownership, and user benefit are more internalized and self-centered principles (Birchall, 2005). In the

---

[1] Definition of The International Cooperative Alliance (2005).

© The Author(s), under exclusive license to Springer Nature Switzerland AG 2023
A. S. Gundogdu, *Food Security, Affordable Housing, and Poverty*, Palgrave Studies in Islamic Banking, Finance, and Economics, https://doi.org/10.1007/978-3-031-27689-7_5

end, broadly defined other principles are also held by other organizations, and cooperatives are based on principles of being user-controlled, user-owned, and distributing benefits to its users equitably (Barton, 1989). Equitability principles suggest that a member farmer who delivered 10% of volume would receive 10% of net earnings after deducting processing, handling, and marketing costs. The business model boosts farmers' income directly or by reducing the cost of the service received indirectly. Such patronage dividends help boost farmers' income directly or by reducing the effective cost of the goods and services provided with the business-at-cost principle (Barton, 1989).

From a historical perspective, the linking commodity between agriculture and industry has been cotton. Cotton processing for fabric production was the sparking point of industrial revaluation in the nineteenth century and the transatlantic slave trade. Enabling indigenous people of West Africa to produce cotton in their homeland and sell in Fair Trade should have been the course rather than enslaving them to work in the cotton fields of foreigners in the Americas. Producing crops for industry enables many farmers to easily access hard currencies, which can assure food security by making it possible to purchase inputs to cultivate staple foods. Availing funds for cash crop cultivation would enable the generation of steady hard currency to sustain the farming cycle from seeding to harvest. This, however, should occur in an environment devoid of price volatility due to speculation in the form of conventional financial derivatives. Unlike East Africa, West African countries were more diligent in restoring cotton cooperative structures. The relative success of West African cotton cooperatives in sustaining the business line indicates the added value of the cooperative business model.

Cooperatives with sound management practices can play an important role by providing financing at a lower rate, discounted input provision, processing and storage of crops, and enhanced profit margin on crops sold. Cooperatives are established by the people that eventually become members. Usually, these people come together when the market fails to provide the needed enabling environment to produce adequate goods or services at affordable prices and acceptable quality. Such members are looking for ways to enhance economic opportunity by strengthening bargaining power in input provision and output sale, providing access to markets and needed services and products, including financing. All this should occur on a competitive basis. In this way, cooperatives aim to reduce costs, manage risks, and improve income opportunities.

The primary motivations of farmers in establishing cooperatives are to generate higher profits by procuring inputs and services at a lower cost and by accessing better output prices in markets that were not previously accessible (Barton, 2000).

The instrumentality of cooperatives can substantially contribute to economic development. Cooperatives' most successful and extensive use has been in Europe and North America in the last century (Barton, 2000). The cooperatives come in different forms: producer, consumer, worker, or service. There are three types of agricultural cooperatives (Cropp & Ingalsbe, 1989):

- **Farm supply cooperatives**: these purchase in volumes farm supplies and inputs such as fertilizer, seed, petroleum products, chemicals, and farm equipment and distribute them to farmers.
- **Service cooperatives**: provide services like trucking, warehousing, ginning, credit, and insurance.
- **Marketing cooperatives**: sell the farm products for a better price with bargaining.

Approaches that used to be relevant for Europe and North America in the last century are still viable alternatives for developing regional agribusiness in emerging economies. These approaches are particularly relevant for smallholder farmers characterized by the lack of technological innovations, low production scale, and market manipulations (Leite et al., 2021). Cooperatives can help smallholder farmers survive by supporting their activities and providing a platform to engage in economic empowerment, Islamic microfinance, and programs.

Cotton Cooperative and Financing[2]

The cotton industry is the leading foreign currency earner and source of employment for many countries in West Africa. Framers in the region's rural areas benefit a lot from selling cottonseed. Consequently, it is vital to ensure that cottonseed production is supported to alleviate the region's poverty. The part of cottonseed production that requires the most support is post-harvest cottonseed processing until the commodity is

---

[2] Refers to the authors own work experience.

ready for export. This chapter will present a creative method of the financial needs of entities involved in the cottonseed post-harvest processes while mitigating the risks inherent in the Islamic structured trade finance design. SOFITEX will be employed as a case study. It is a state-controlled firm in Burkina Faso involved in ginning, transportation, warehousing, and shipping of agro commodities. This chapter will use the case study to illustrate how to finance the agricultural sector beginning from the procurement of inputs to selling and exporting, using Islamic finance instruments. It will also illustrate how to use commodities in a warehouse to guarantee a transaction instead of a sovereign, mortgage, or bank guarantee. The chapter analyzes the existing Islamic structured finance design for SOFITEX to provide a clear comprehension of the subject matter.

> SOFITEX was established in 1979 as a public-sector liability company. Its principal shareholders incorporated it: the Compagnie Francaise pour le Developpement du Textiles (CFDT) and the government of Burkina Faso. It would later grow into one of the biggest cotton companies in West Africa. Its closest rival was Mali's Compagnie Malienne pour le Developpement des Textiles (CMDT). SOFITEX has a monopoly in the cotton processing sector in Burkina Faso until 2004. The company was responsible for the complete commercial and industrial activities related to exporting cotton and ensuring the social development of populations in rural areas. In the West African region, SOFITEX is the only firm with a seed production facility (delinting units) that help improve the quality of seedcotton for improved yield and more resistant varieties.

After evaluating the structure at SOFTEX, this book will suggest a new design for better accommodating the company's financing needs. In the real-life case presented in this chapter, two contracts exist. The first is the Mudaraba contract between the Mudarab and Rabb al-Mal, involving the delegation of authority for the undertakings of this financing operation. The other is the Murabaha contract between the beneficiary and Mudarab. This contract stipulates conditions under which Mudarab purchases cotton fiber from the cotton producers to sell to the beneficiaries based on a predetermined markup. In contrast to many Murabaha transactions, selling to the beneficiary does not occur instantaneously. Instead, it occurs at the time of the export.

Typically, banks playing a part in international trade finance depend on the balance sheet analysis and find government guarantees or creditworthiness assessment for potential clients comforting. In such cases, the primary way of determining security is through tangible assets. Consequently, in the majority of cases, real estate forms the best collateral in such cases. In the developing world, traders have large credit requirements compared to their equity. This is a reality acknowledged by the International Trade Centre (ITC), whose surveys show that banks often ask for collateral in the form of physical assets equal to 150% of the trade finance facility's value in developing economies.

In most cases, potential traders do not have a good credit history, capital base, or access to government guarantees due to the obligations of governments to the IMF. Typically, traders are requested to show that they have made a profit in the last three years after requesting financing. Local bank guarantees are approached with a certain level of assistance when determining whether an individual is eligible for clean financing. This leads to only a few large credit-worthy traders actively participating in the markets of developing countries. Credit providers are cautious when extending trade finance on an unsecured basis to traders in developing countries because such traders are prone to high default rates.

Privatization and globalization are the other factors giving rise to more structured finance. Privatization has seen many trading activities moving away from the influence of the state into the ambit of private business. While private companies often back sales to the private sector, those of government entities remain backed by a government guarantee. However, these guarantees do not seem to mean much in regions like sub-Saharan Africa. Looking at the political and economic situation in these regions like sub-Saharan Africa, it becomes clear that it is not always easy to forecast the future. This makes companies doing business in the region apprehensive and pile stringent requirements on anyone looking for capital to invest. This makes it challenging to penetrate the markets using traditional approaches and stimulate economic development. One method that some have looked toward regarding solving the challenges is structured trade finance (STF). The STF's main objective involves meeting the borrower's needs regarding issues like maturity and repayment schedule. For the credit provider, STF attempts to meet default risk and repatriation issues.

Consequently, the STF approach does not come with any standardized structured trade finance deals as it seeks to meet the specific needs of various parties. This explains the proliferation of a range of structures and innovative financing methods to deal with the risk of losses and gauge the possibility of losses linked to the financing of agricultural transactions which has become a crucial feature of the development agenda. Some multilateral development agencies are involved in attempts to come up with better-structured trade finance deals. Examples of these institutions include the Islamic Development Bank, African Development Bank, and the World Bank.[3] However, an analysis of efforts in the Islamic context shows that very little has been done when factoring in sustainability parameters. Most of the interventions ended up in racks and ruins.

WHAT IS STRUCTURED TRADE FINANCE[4]

STF involves how funded, and non-funded capital solutions are delivered outside the traditional fallback on securities. When structured finance is employed, the focus is no longer on the borrower's strength but on the fundamental cash flow generated out of the structure that improves secure financing.[5] STF is cross-border trade finance in developing markets where beneficiaries do not have sufficient financial strength to qualify for traditional financing. In the arrangement, repayment is devised as liquidating a flow of commodities. Nonetheless, this approach has some possible weaknesses that have resulted in a poor image within the finance community. However, it has been noted that in comparison to other types of investment or lending in emerging markets, STF has shown itself to be able to survive under the most challenging environments.[6]

As can be discerned from the definition, STFs focus on externalizing or mitigating the identified risks related to transactions with parties that have the potential to bear such risks. For this reason, the main concern is identifying the role of different parties regarding their ability to tolerate risk in the funding and reimbursement phase. Trade finance has many inherent risks. An excellent example of such risks is the volatility in the price of commodities. This can become a huge concern for financiers dealing with forms of producing, processing, and trading commodities. Nonetheless,

---

[3] Operations implemented within the framework of the Africa Trade Facilitation Project (ATFP) targeting Africa Trade Insurance (ATI), Exporters and Importers in COMESA region.

[4] Based on the book "Trade Finance Infrastructure Development Handbook for Economies in Transition (2005)", United Nations Publication.

[5] World Bank Institute definition.

[6] John MacNamara (2008), "Structured trade and commodity finance: What can go wrong and how to avoid it", Woodhead Publishing Limited.

evidence from practice shows that even when conditions are hostile, STF can still deliver benefits for both the beneficiaries and financiers. In relation to this, let us briefly focus on warehouse receipt financing and export receivable models for mitigating risk in STF for the case presented in this book.

Financing Based on Warehouse Receipt

The exporters make a firm commitment to the credit provider that they will reimburse the credit provider through a sale of existing produces which is not seen by credit providers as solid. Nonetheless, the goods under the custodianship of a third party (the warehouse operator) could form a basis for secure collateral, considering that the commodities have not been pledged in the past and the credit provider reserves the first call on the goods where need be.

When the goods arrive from the producer, the warehouse operator issues a receipt in warehouse receipt financing. That receipt becomes the guarantee regarding the goods' grade, quantity, and quality as the foundation of the financing arrangement. The producer can use the receipt as collateral when asking for financing from a financial institution. For the credit providers, the receipt could be used as a fallback guarantee where it happens that payment is not received. Considering the character of the transactions, the legal framework concerning warehouse receipts should be well established in a developing country so that the developers can enjoy the full benefits of this type of financing. For sure, the existence of Licensed Warehouses would substantially add value to the collateral management and mitigate legal risk.

Financing Based on Export Receivable

As noted in the name, financing relies on the payments anticipated from off-takers after exporting the commodities. This allows exporters to use their future trade flows to raise self-liquidating financing cost-effectively. On the other hand, it presents an advantage to credit providers who can externalize country risk by receiving payments into an escrow account, out of the country, and credit risks by assigning export contracts and receivables. It must be noted that the credit provider still maintains the security of the physical commodity under local law. Assignment of Receivables in an escrow account out of the country would mitigate country risk.

Here, the leading objective is to illustrate how to use Islamic finance instruments in STF deals as an alternative to conventional financing. Before Mudarab developed this product, conventional financing did not have an alternative in the region. At that point, the financing would only start after the cotton fiber has arrived in the warehouse. Upgrading the structure facilitates a situation where the beneficiary can get financing right at the start of a pre-harvesting period. This chapter will go beyond the prevailing structure and suggest a Salam contract for complete supply chain financing, beginning with input financing. Sharing these insights aims to trigger the development of literature in the area in pursuit of availing more funds for food security.[7]

In the next section, Burkina Faso's cotton industry is introduced together with SOFITEX. The other section focuses on explaining the prevailing Islamic structure and how Salam can be the method for upgrading the structure for complete supply chain financing. The final section delivers the conclusion.

Financing Facility Structure

Considering the risk associated with activities after the harvest, conventional financiers are often hesitant to make finance available until cotton fiber reaches a certain point they believe is safe. However, regarding Islamic finance, there is always room for negotiating the risks for farmers and ginners: SOFITEX and financiers as a way of boosting cotton production in the country.

Farmers who lack financing facilities suffer two risks: production (crop) and late payment risk. The leading risk for producers is late payment for their produce, which leads to storage cost risk. The cotton financing facility proposed in this book aims to deal with the risk of non-payment for farmers by designing the transaction so that farmers receive their payment upfront at the ginning level.

In the current structure of Burkina Faso's cotton sector, SOFITEX is the defector credit guarantor during the production period beginning at

---

[7] *Mudaraba* is a special kind of partnership where one partner provides the capital (*rabb-al-mal*) to the other (mudarab) for investment in a commercial enterprise.

the phase when the letter of credit is opened to allow for the importation of inputs like fertilizer to the end where off-takers make payment. Therefore, the company is involved from the pre-harvest to the post-harvest period. In such a situation, the financial risk is high, considering that the process could last more than two and a half years. However, the input recovery risk is low due to the connection between input supply and seed cotton marketing. Additionally, farmers have joint liability through agricultural cooperatives in Burkina Faso. Nonetheless, the risks for ginners like SOFITEX are linked to buying the seedcotton from the farmers as a post-harvest activity.

Regarding selling fiber to off-takers, the ginners counterbalance the risk inherent in fluctuating exchange rates by pricing their produce in Euros. Considering that off-takers are paid among established buyers, the contract performance risk is moderate, and the contract performance risk is low. If prices drop between the contract date and the shipment data, delayed payment and defaults by off-takers escalate. Ginners do not usually apply to carry charges to late shipments, and the contracts do not factor in storage costs for late shipments.

On behalf of Rabb al-Mal, Mudarab reduces the financial burden on SOFITEX in the post-harvest period of the flow by entering into a Murabaha agreement. Based on that agreement, once the seedcotton has been processed, Mudarab would purchase the cotton fiber upfront and sell it to SOFITEX with a markup during the exporting period. The Murabaha agreements details will be explained in the sections that follow.

Financier's Security Structure

Notwithstanding the reality that the finance industry is based on the assumption that financiers will always accept a certain level of risk, it is also vital that they find ways of mitigating that risk. Some of the methods through which risk can be mitigated are presented below.

1. In keeping with the model provided by Mudarab, the government of Burkina Faso issues a letter of comfort.
2. Mudarab receives a pledge of the cotton contracts with pre-approved off-takers from the financed cotton company for an amount equivalent to 110% of the financing approved.
3. Pledge of the nominated debt service account (Escrow account) opened with an acceptable financial institution. This account will

hold all amounts from the pledged exports and will only be used when repaying the provided facility.
4. A pledge of the physical cotton worth 115% of the facility sum created from the financed cotton company, by way of warehouse receipt issued by a collateral management company acceptable to financiers, on a volume of cotton fiber equal to the financing outstanding.
5. Regarding repayment, the primary source is assigning the export receivables from the harvested cotton. This amount is paid into the Escrow account opened outside Burkina Faso and is acceptable to the Mudarab. The beneficiary and Mudarab will agree on the mechanism for the assignment. The cotton fiber export calendar made available by the beneficiary will be crucial to this agreement.

The Escrow account mitigates the country and foreign exchange risk for the financiers. Regarding the physical control of the commodity, the warehouse receipt constitutes a guarantee to the financiers. On the other hand, the assurance that the repayment of the financing facility will be received as per schedule is given by the export contract. The following sections present the implementation schedule, providing a more wide-ranging comprehension of the financiers' security package.

Schedule of Implementation and Security Package

Ahead of the pronouncement regarding effectiveness, an Escrow account, mainly in US$ or Euro, is opened at a financial institution acceptable to the Mudarab. That account is opened in the name of the Mudarab. If the account is not in the Mudarab, it will have to be pledged to the Mudarab. This is the account through which some of the export receivables will be deposited, and they will later constitute the source of repayment for the financial institutions that participated. Table 5.1 presents the time of activities and their owners, covering from Quarter-2 of the "Year (t)" to Quarter-3 of "Year (t+1)". Table 5.1 presents the schedule of the financing cycle.

In working with the beneficiary (SOFITEX), Mudarab nominates a bank/agent to play the role of the facility agent. This agent will represent Mudarab and all other role players. The agent is expected to receive and complete all realistic checks on specific documents with regard to relevance, accuracy, and authenticity when verifying:

Table 5.1 Schedule of cotton financing cycle

Operation	Q 2–(t)	Q 3–(t)	Q 4–(t)	Q 1–(t+1)	Q 2–(t+1)	Q 3–(t+1)
Distribution of inputs to farmers (SOFITEX)	▓					
Sowing of seeds (Farmers)	▓	▓				
Rainy season		▓	▓			
Harvest (Farmers)			▓	▓		
Collection (Cooperatives)				▓	▓	
Disbursement of facility (Financiers)				▓	▓	
Ginning (SOFITEX)					▓	▓
Export (SOFITEX)						▓
Export proceeds (Off-Takers)						▓

- The list of pre-approved off-takers
- Sales contracts with amounts of no less than 110% of the financing amount.
- Insurance policies containing the loss payee clause
- All off-takers are notified of the pledge
- The notified off-takers confirm receipt and acceptance of the written notification to pay the Escrow account.

An agreement is reached with the Mudarab regarding a list of pre-approved off-takers. The off-takers are selected based on the standing and longstanding business relationship with SOFETEX and other ginners. Once the off-takers have been selected, contracts are signed with them as early as September of the year (t). The signed contracts form part of the agreement that the Mudarab will be paid an aggregate value of 110% of the amount disbursed. The off-takers officially recognize the assignment of sales contracts and agree that they will make payment into the chosen Escrow account, which is generally called the collection A/C. This happens via that notice of assignment forwarded by the facility agent.

A collateral management monitoring contract (CMMC) is signed toward the end of the year (usually in September but no later than October). The signatories to that contract will be the Mudarab of Rabb al-Mal, SOFITEX, and a collateral manager. SOFITEX is responsible for organizing and maintaining a wide-ranging transport and storage insurance with a reputable insurance company. In that policy, the Mudarab must be defined as the loss payee before the fund is disbursed.

When the GPCs, on behalf of farmers, have collected the cotton from Farmers, an agreement is signed between SOFITEX and the Mudarab stipulating that the latter will buy the cotton from the GPCs' upfront before selling it to SOFITEX based on a deferred payment with a markup at the time of the exports.[8] Based on a call option described below, the beneficiary receives the facility in trenches:

(a) **Tranche 1—At the ginning level**

$$75\% \times \left\{ \begin{array}{l} \text{Ginning Outturn} \times \text{Quantity of Seed Cotton} \\ \times \text{Average Price} \end{array} \right\}$$

(b) **Tranche 2—Upon shipment of cotton fiber**

$$85\% \left\{ \left(\begin{array}{l} \text{Effective Price} \\ \times \text{Quantity of Cotton Fibre} \end{array} \right) \right\} - \text{Disb. Tranche 1}$$

OR

$$85\% \left\{ \left(\begin{array}{l} \text{Average Price} \\ \times \text{Quantity of Cotton Fibre} \end{array} \right) \right\} - \text{Disb. Tranche 1}$$

where:

Ginning Outturn represents the average ginning rate of 0.42 (42%) into the fiber (Sofitex process the raw cotton to separate seeds to have cotton fiber bales).

Quantity of seedcotton denotes the quantity of seedcotton transported at the ginning mills.

The average cotton price signifies the lowest average price of the cotton market prices or the average cotton market of the export contracts.

Effective Price is the price stipulated in the sales contracts pledged to the Mudarab signed between SOFITEX and pre-approved off-takers.

---

[8] SOFITEX act as agent of the Mudarab in Murabaha Agreement.

Quantity of Cotton Fiber stands for the quantity of cotton fiber supplied after the ginning process.

Regarding the payment trenches, the basic idea is that the financing amount would always be lower than the market value of the commodity held at the ginning warehouse (seedcotton) and the port warehouse (cotton fiber bale). This implies that the Mudarab, when disbursing the financing facility, considers the market value of seedcotton and the cotton fiber bale in the warehouse.

Taking the role of being an agent of the Mudarab, SOFITEX collects the seedcotton from the GPCs to its ginning mills. The CMM supervises the process. At the SOFITEX ginnery, the seedcotton is processes before being graded, packed into bales, and stored. In storage, the CMM is responsible for the commodity while it remains at the SOFITEX premise or gets ready to be transported to the ports of export's terminal houses. At every moment the CM reports that they have received cotton bales, they issue a warehouse receipt (WR), which is the basis of control over the physical cotton. As the time for implementing the corresponding exports draws closer, the bales with the cotton fiber are loaded into containers. Supervised by the CMM, the freight forwarder prepares the export documentation based on standard business practices. As required, an application is submitted to the facility agent. This agent completes the due diligence based on the requirements of the security package.

Following every shipment, the freight forwarder makes the shipping documents available to the facility agent, who checks and verifies them before they are submitted. This happens with the collection order provided to the collecting banks to facilitate negotiation and payment by off-takers. The payment is made into the nominated Escrow account, and utility proceeds in the Escrow account will be committed for as long as any amount remains due. The beneficiary, SOFITEX, reserves the right to draw any access amounts remaining in the Escrow account. If the maturity date has arrived and the Mudarab has not received payment for any sums under the facility, on the first demand, the beneficiary is expected to pay the amount or any shortfall owed to the Mudarab and any other costs, and penalties levied on behalf of Rabb al-Mal.

Collateral Management

The company responsible for managing collateral plays a pivotal role in transactions. Therefore, it is required that a CM of good standing able to facilitate processes across all ports in West Africa is appointed. Such a CM should also have experience in collateral activities linked to cotton. The CM, SOFITEX, and the Mudarab immediately sign a collateral management and monitoring contract (CMMC). Among others, the CM will take charge of the following:

- Monitoring the arrival of trucks transporting the seedcotton to the ginning mills.
- Supervise the weighbridge processes involving the weighing of the trucks carrying the seedcotton.
- Manage the issuing of the weighing ticket for every truckload arriving at the ginning mill.
- Before requesting disbursement from the facility manager, the CMM reviews documents.
- Provide a storage certificate with details about the weight, quantity, and quality of cotton bales, presented in the form of a warehouse receipt.
- Reconciling the exiting from the factories to those received in the stores at the harbor warehouse.

The process of monitoring the ginning process, production of cotton, and packing it into bales is monitored by the CM as soon as the commodity arrives in the mills. The nominated CM takes custody of the cotton bales as soon as they arrive at the premises of SOFITEX, the ginner, and the warehouses leased by the CM at the port of export. Concerning the pledge of the cotton stock, the Mudarab ranks first. The CM makes available professional indemnity insurance covering the risks linked with deterioration, loss, or decrease in the value of the collateral, expenses incurred as a result of negligence, willful misconduct, or default, by either the employees or the CM in performing the Collateral Management and Monitoring Agreement (CMMA).

When the CM receives cotton bales, a WR is issued, which is the approach through which control over the physical cotton is maintained. On account of all role players, the WRs are pledged to the Mudarab. The WRs are issued under SOFITEX on behalf of the Mudarab. The Mudarab is eligible to receive the WR for the amount of cotton equal to the value of the weight at the average price, as indicated by the export contracts entered into with pre-approved off-takers. It is always expected that the WR value should be above the amount due. It is also the responsibility of the CM to determine the precise quantity of goods and if there are any that have been damaged before the WRs are issued.

Cotton bales are kept at the SOFTEX premises in various locations and will continuously be transported to specific ports by trucks or transit storage before they are shipped. The CM is responsible for issuing bales of transfer and delivery notice statements whenever a transfer occurs. The CM is also responsible for reconciling quantities transported from factories to those received in the warehouse stores at the harbor.

SOFITEX could ask the facility manager of Mudarab for authorization to release the commodity for shipment under the following circumstances:

- When correctly worded, L/Cs are remitted from the pre-approved off-takers, verified by the facility agent nominated by Mudarab.
- Based on official direction (with a copy of the facility agent), providing details regarding quantity, price, loading, shipping line, and destination from the pre-approved off-takers to ship the goods to their intended destination, based on the documentary collection. Based on this arrangement, the facility agent will play the role of the remitting bank for the presentation of shipping documents and the collection order to the collecting bank so that payment can be made and the shipping documents are released.

After every shipment, the CM provides the documents to the facility agent for checking and verification before they are submitted to the off-takers' banks for negotiation and payment. As was earlier indicated, an Escrow account is used to receive the payment. After repayment is paid in full, all WRs that remain under the facility manager's custody would be submitted to SOFITEX or other ginners following endorsement. When the full payment of balances has been made, any balance in the nominated Escrow account would be transferred to the account designated by SOFITEX.

Assessment of the Structure

From the SOFITEX, the loan seeker beneficiary, perspective, much of the advantage gets lost because of the need to pay money into an Escrow account upfront. The entire amount of export receivables is maintained in an account, even though SOFITEX receives the interest revenue until the facility is repaid in full. The prevailing structure could be revised as illustrated in the case presented in the box below:

> Wen farmers deliver their seedcotton for ginning, the seedcotton is processed into cotton fiber. This cotton fiber is purchased on behalf of Rabb al Mal on behalf of Mudarab. Let's work on the case that the weight of purchased cotton fiber is 70,000,000 kg. Only 85% of the available cotton fiber value will be purchased, at a prevailing market price of 1 Euro. Therefore, the cotton fiber purchased by Mudarab on behalf of Rabb al Mall will cost Euro 59,500,000 (70,000,000 × 1 × 0.85). Let's now assume that three months following the purchase of the cotton, the beneficiary decides to sell 20,000,000 kg of cotton fiber. If purchased at the price from three months back, the Mudarab on behalf of Rabb al Mall, will sell this for Euro 17,297,500 to the beneficiary (purchase price for 3 month back × 1 + 0.07/4). It is vital to remember that 0.07 is the supposed predetermined amount per year for purposes of illustration. Every time a sale is made, it is only this part of the export receivable that will be requested to be transferred to an escrow account. Any profit made by the beneficiary as a consequence of increased prices and export sales profit margin, will be kept in the account.

Generally, it needs to be noted that the existing Murabaha structure is not an appropriate fit. A much more suitable approach for this type of operation would be Salam. If we were to categorize the cotton production process into the pre-harvest and post-harvest phases, the structure we will design here targets the financing of post-harvest activities. Therefore, to ensure greater effectiveness, the financing needs to be available right from the start of the cycle in the pre-harvest period when farmers need to procure inputs like seed, urea, pesticides, and fertilizer. This ensures that farmers have all the necessary resources when the production cycle begins.

Working with the cooperatives, the process will begin with the pre-ordering of inputs. These would then be distributed based on the crop agenda. The distribution will be managed through GPCs and cooperatives. Under the supervision of the CM, the distribution will be monitored, adding up and weighing the actual movement of inputs from the providers of inputs to farmers. The idea is that individual farmers will be paying less with bulk purchases of inputs. However, the payment will only be collected after the harvest by deducting the farmers' sales earnings. Farmers will deliver their seedcotton to their cooperatives, which issues them a delivery ticket, which will be matched with the input deliveries from the beginning of the planning season. This will make it possible to deduct the correct input costs. The cooperatives deliver the seedcotton to the cotton gins. Here, the cotton is kept in warehouses under the custodianship of a CM. This is the phase at which the CM issues a WR for the seedcotton in cotton fiber equivalent terms, depending on the processing ratio of each gin. This will be the basis on which the Mudarab takes ownership of the seedcotton.

In the following steps, the Mudarab reserves the right to choose between different financing approaches: Islamic joint venture, Musharakah, Islamic manufacturing contract, and Istisna. This type of short-term transaction may not be suitable for Istisna. Pre-harvest financing would lower the financing liability of two and a half years for the ginning company (SOFITEX) and the public sector while facilitating the country's much-needed foreign exchange earnings. As an illustration, Annex-II presents a simplified price calculation for the Salam agreement.

In managing the financing facility, the most important aspect to keep in mind is to maintain total control of the quality of the commodity. Therefore, a reputable insurance provider must be identified during storage. The role of the CM as a quantity and quality assurance also remains important. If the CM were to be involved in any misconduct or default, the whole structure would crumble. For this reason, Mudarab needs to alleviate the risk shifted to the CM by ensuring that the CM has professional indemnity insurance provided by a reputable service provider. Under the insurance structure and coverage presented here, making it possible for all the role players to handle risk, some other Islamic structures can be conducted successfully to alleviate poverty and make the proposed approach sustainable by ensuring timely repayment of financing amount back to the credit providers.

The real-life case presented above illustrates the superior role played by Salam for the complete supply chain financing beginning at the input phase for the cotton sector. In doing this, it becomes possible for us to create benefits for various parties. Based on the case presented in this chapter, it can be noted that Rabb al-Mal has access to liquidity even though it does not have expertise in STF or the cotton sector. Based on this structure, Rabb al-Mal can place its funds in a secure financing transaction with a higher yield than regular financing transactions. Mudarab uses its intellectual prowess to design a safe transaction and attain the Mudarab fee. The beneficiary gains a partner financing stream production process and alleviates some of its financial challenges. Farmers enjoy the benefit of getting timely inputs through Salam for pre-harvest activities. Immediately, they collect the monetary reward for their effort in growing the crop as soon as it has been delivered at the ginner's warehouse. This is an improvement compared to a situation where they wait for between six and eight months from export receivables to buy the inputs they need. Providing input to farmers in a timely manner is a factor to contribute to food security. This gets even more critical in the years when input and output price fluctuation despair farmers. Managing the presented structure would be more prevalent should we incorporate licensed warehouses operated by third parties.

Any proposal on food security and affordable housing would not be sustainable should the issue of enabling infrastructure is not resolved. The infrastructure is needed not only to provide licensed warehouses to ensure proper warehousing but also to irrigate land, transport agricultural commodities from railroads/roads and ports to markets, and provide the social infrastructure of education and health to housing communities. The current approach to infrastructure development is far from filling the bill for food security and affordable housing. The next chapter provides an Islamic perspective of infrastructure for equitable services in rural and urban communities.

ANNEX-I EXPORT CASH FLOW

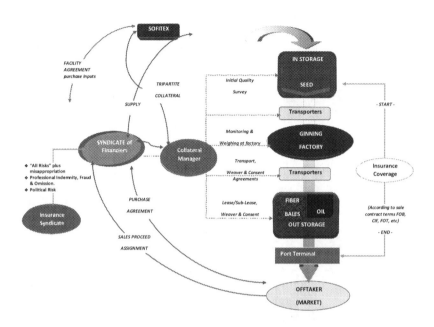

ANNEX-II SALAM PRICE CALCULATION

Question: How is price in Salam contract for structured cotton trade financing structured?

Fact: Predetermined markup is 7% per annum.

Time	March 1, 2010	December 1, 2010	February 1, 2011	March 1, 2011
Point for Scenarios	1	2	3	4
Cotton fiber price per Kg	1 Euro	0.9 Euro	1.2 Euro	1.3 Euro
Cotton fiber price per tons	1000 Euro	900 Euro	1200 Euro	1300 Euro

First Scenario

1. MUDARAB disburses Euro 10 million, by which MUDARAB can buy 10,000 tons of cotton fiber at the current price of 1 Euro/Kg from the market. The ginner agrees to provide 30,000 tons of cotton fiber in December 1, 2010 under Salam contract for the disbursement amount.
2. MUDARAB assumes pledge of 30,000 tons of cotton fiber in warehouses monitored by CMMC.
3. The ginner asks for the release of 20,000 tons of cotton fiber. MUDARAB receives only the following amount in an escrow account to release the cotton fiber (MUDARAB sales the cotton fiber of 20,000 tons for):

    $(10,000/30,000) \times 20,000 \times 1,000$ Euro $\times (1 + (0.07 \times (11/12))) =$ $6666.667 \times 1,000$ Euro $\times 1.064167 = 7,094,444$ Euro

    Markup $= 7,094,444 - 6,666,667$
    Markup $= 427,777$ Euro

4. The ginner asks for the release of 10,000 tons of cotton fiber. MUDARAB receives only the following amount in an escrow account to release the cotton fiber (MUDARAB sales the cotton fiber of 10,000 tons for):

    $(10,000/30,000) \times 10,000 \times 1,000$ Euro $\times (1.07) =$ $3333.333 \times 1,000$ Euro $\times 1.07 = 7,094,444$ Euro $= 3,566,667$ Euro

    Markup $= 3,566,667 - 3,333,333$
    Markup $= 233,333$ Euro

    Total markup for the first scenario $= 427,777 + 233,333 = 661,111$ Euro

Second Scenario

1. The ginner asks for the release of 30,000 tons of cotton fiber. MUDARAB receives the following amount in an escrow account to release the cotton fiber (MUDARAB sales the cotton fiber of

30,000 tons for):

$$(10,000/30,000) \times 30,000 \times 1,000 \text{ Euro} \times (1.07) =$$
$$10,000 \times 1,000 \text{ Euro} \times 1.07 = 10,700,000 \text{ Euro}$$

On March 1, 2010 Euro 10,000,000 disbursed and a year later amount repaid back with Euro 700,000 markup

Total markup for the second scenario = 700,000 Euro

REFERENCES

Barton, D. (2000). *What is a cooperative?* [Unpublished paper, Kansas State University, USA].
Barton, D. G. (1989). What is a cooperative? In D. Cobia (Ed.), *Cooperatives in agriculture* (pp. 1–20). Prentice-Hall, Inc.
Birchall, J. (2005). Principles ten years on. *International Cooperative Alliance, 2, 98*(2), 45–63. http://www.ica.coop/ (accessed on September 1, 2005).
Cropp, R., & Ingalsbe, G. (1989). *Structure and scope of agricultural cooperatives.* Cobia, Cooperatives in agriculture. Prentice-Hall Inc.
Essama-nssah, B., Samakéand, I., & Walliser, J. (2008). Burkina Faso: A macroeconomic approach to analyze cotton sector reform. http://siteresources.worldbank.org/INTPSIA/Resources/490023-1120841262639/ch3_burkinafaso.pdf on 29 December 2008.
Leite. A., Padilha, M., & Erlaine, B. (2021). Cooperation challenges in agricultural cooperatives. *Revista de Administração da UFSM, 14*(4).
MacNamara, J. (2008). *Structured trade and commodity finance: What can go wrong and how to avoid it.* Woodhead Publishing Limited.
Ortmann, G. F., & King, R. P. (2007). Agricultural cooperatives I: History, theory and problems. *Agrekon, 46*(1).
Trade Finance Infrastructure Development Handbook for Economies in Transition (2005) United Nations Publication.

CHAPTER 6

Enabling Infrastructure

"Smaller is better."

There is euphoria for infrastructure investment among politicians, project undertakers, and financial institutions. For politicians, in addition to rent-seeking, infrastructure investment is an excellent way of gaining popular support, especially where project assets are able to deliver economic and social services within the office term and repayments are out with the term, thus becoming a problem for their successors. It is not only the delivery of services with project assets that attract public support but also the job opportunities created. Besides, FX loan entry into the country helps with the balance of payments and supports the FX reserves of the Central Bank of the country, with the potential of local currency appreciation to enhance the wealth of the local population with increased non-tradables prices, such as real estate, and opportunities to import tradables, such as luxury automobiles. That is why there is a relationship between infrastructure investment and economic development in the short term, while in the long term this relationship is not there (Haidar et al., 2012). The same holds for the effect of infrastructure investment on income inequality: in the long term, income inequality becomes even worse with public investment (Chatterjee & Turnovsky, 2012). What is beautiful in the short term often becomes ugly in the longer term—a problem to be dealt with by those who come later. Project undertakers and financial institutions get lucrative business opportunities for which

---

© The Author(s), under exclusive license to Springer Nature Switzerland AG 2023
A. S. Gundogdu, *Food Security, Affordable Housing, and Poverty*, Palgrave Studies in Islamic Banking, Finance, and Economics, https://doi.org/10.1007/978-3-031-27689-7_6

the risk is mitigated with government guarantees or undertakings—again, liability for posterity and benefit for incumbents.

Regardless of proof to the contrary, infrastructure investment is proposed as the champion of everything. There is an assumption that infrastructure investment leads to economic growth and, in turn, that economic growth takes care of poverty, and hence food security and shelter. In reality, however, regardless of massive infrastructure investment, the issue of poverty is still there. Studies on infrastructure investment, economic growth, and poverty alleviation show a positive relationship between infrastructure investment and economic growth (Luo & Xu, 2018).[1] Despite this positive correlation, it is better to be cautious about the claim that infrastructure investment leads to economic growth. The relationship might be opposite, or there might be a simultaneity effect as well. For instance, in the 1990s Japan squandered US$ 29 billion to build seventeen bridges for three expressways to connect Shikoku to the main island of Honshu. The era is known as the "lost decade of Japan" (Woetzel & Pohl, 2014). A similar positive correlation is present between infrastructure investment and income inequality (Timilisina et al., 2020). There are studies that suggest infrastructure investment paves the way for economic growth in developing countries, unlike the situation in developed countries (Esfahani & Ramirez, 2003; Sanchez-Robles, 1998). The idea is that, for developing countries, infrastructure investment upgrades economic structure and connects local economies to the global value chain based on comparative advantages of the geography, thus powering local businesses (Luo & Xu, 2018). However, there is a need to be cautious before assuming infrastructure as the savior.

The global value chain concept is based on providing an enabling environment to big multinational corporations along with enabling business partnerships and market access in local economies. In the old days of colonialism, colonial powers were used to invest in roads, railways, and ports to have access to local natural resources. The concept of a global value chain suggests that countries invest in infrastructure with loans from financial markets: debt being paid by local communities and market access gained by big multinational corporations (Diallo & Gundogdu, 2021). The idea was that good public infrastructure increases the return for firms

---

[1] Infrastructure contribution to economic growth and productivity can be through the following: crowd-in other productive inputs, lowering transaction costs, increasing total factor productivity, and lowering production costs.

and lowers the barriers to firms' entry (Porter, 2000). However, studies suggest that even local companies that supply multinationals are worse off because of diminishing profit margins and diminishing margins for labor in both developing and developed countries, leaving multinationals as the main beneficiaries (Choi et al., 2019; World Bank, 2019).

Infrastructure investment does not function properly for international development. However, it may pave the way for economic growth without exacerbating income inequality if checks and balances are applied to ensure sustainability. The solution is to avoid adverse selection and moral hazard with infrastructure investment and embed sustainability measures for project design. The issue of adverse selection and moral hazard can be addressed using infrastructure prioritization frameworks (IPFs) that incorporate extensive feasibility analysis based on net present value (NPV) and social cost–benefit analysis (SCBA) (Marcelo et al., 2016). There are several methodological frameworks for prioritizing infrastructure projects, yet these are not substitutes for political negotiation (Andres et al., 2015). Unfortunately, project prioritization is not based on a systematic appraisal but on politics, on professional judgment without clear principles underpinning selection, and on loose qualitative assessments (Petrie, 2010). Even if we assume prioritization and selection frameworks can work, infrastructure investment cannot yield the desired result of poverty alleviation as long as there exists the issue of sustainability—in the form of assets at rack and ruins or failure in the financial management of the project assets in the end. Consistently, we see unscrupulous politicians, financial institutions, and project undertakers who take advantage of the public for their personal benefit. Indirect taxes are collected from the poor and resources are transferred to big corporations; unlike assumption, mega infrastructure assets benefit those above the middle-class segment of society, but not the poor at the bottom (Khandker et al., 2014). Indeed, there is limited information available on affordability and access for the poor; hence, a major obstacle still exists when attempting to establish a cause-and-effect relationship between infrastructure development and poverty alleviation (Calderon & Serven, 2014). On the other hand, it is well acknowledged that infrastructure investment enables firms to thrive because the new infrastructure services are more reliable and do not cause disruption (Braese et al., 2019). This indicates the importance of the business model in managing project assets to ensure service quality.

Proper maintenance of infrastructure substantially decreases the need for new investment (Kornejew et al., 2019). Maintenance and affordable service charges vis-à-vis financial management of project assets are key factors in ensuring sustainability. To guarantee the effective provision of public services, institutions need to have robust governance structures, with clear assignment of accountabilities, and transparent and reliable financing mechanisms (Acemoglu, 2005). Governance is key to ensuring transparency in decision-making and inhibiting "white elephant" infrastructure investments that satisfy influential interest groups at the expense of people's lives and livelihoods. Having good governance standards means that authorities will allocate more funding to the maintenance of infrastructure, resulting in better reliability and service quality vis-à-vis affordability for service users (Kornejew et al., 2019).

To avoid unfairness and ensure sustainability, certain steps can be taken. First of all, infrastructure investment should not be mediated by commercial banks. Instead, multilateral development banks (MDBs)—which do not have profit maximization concerns and are focused more on long-term social and economic sustainability aspects—should play the role. MDBs have long-standing procurement practices that inhibit unjust enrichment of project undertakers, observe value for money in project selection, consider the affordability of services to be provided, and ensure environmental and social safeguards. The silent feature of MDB involvement should hinder politicians' hidden agendas and/or recklessness. Politicians are not necessarily working against people should the people pressure them to work in their favor, a case is provided in Case Box 6.1.

Case Box 6.1: Jamuna Bridge Project/Bangladesh
In August 1996, World Bank Inspection Panel received a request from a Bangladeshi NGO representing Char People. Char people live on mid-channel islands emerging, as a result of accretion, periodically from the Jamuna River bed. According to complaints, the IDA did not comply with its resettlement, participation of NGOs, and environmental assessment policies. NGO claimed that the initial resettlement plan did not even factor the existence of the Char people. The IDA responded in September 1996 by making reference to an erosion and flood policy adopted by the country. The issue was bridge construction led to permeant flooding of islands and

> the erosion and flooding policy were adopted after the complaint was registered while IDA was drafting a response to the claim. In 1998, World Bank Inspection Panel noted that the erosion and flood action plan despite some remaining problems, the plan mitigated the adverse effect of the project on Char people.
> *Source* Shihata (2000).

Second, the project or asset being developed should be able to pay for itself in the long term without recourse to public sources (Gundogdu, 2019c). Islam is against tax collection-based public finance because tax collection, and transaction tax, in particular, is forbidden (Gundogdu, 2019a). The main concern with such restrictions is that those who control the government can levy a tax on people and then distribute the resources collected to those who are close to and/or support them in power. In most cases, such favors would be in the form of public tenders—including infrastructure projects. Hence, infrastructure investment should not be done with public resources or public tenders. Besides, it would be better to develop assets using MDBs' procurement systems to prohibit corruption.

DEFINITION AND CATEGORIZATION OF INFRASTRUCTURE

If tax resources should not be used to finance infrastructure, how can a society develop key infrastructures such as schools, hospitals, or roads? An Islamic answer can be found in:

1. the hierarchy of Fi'sabilillah spending
2. the definition and categorization of infrastructure.

Fi'sabilillah spending is Islamic charitable spending in a good cause for the sake of Allah. It has a hierarchy of Infak, Sadaqa, Zakat, and Waqf (Gundogdu, 2019b). Infaq is spending on the family to provide food, clothing, and shelter for members, including preparing youngsters for the future through the provision of proper education and training. Once a person is able to fulfill the Infaq obligation, the next stages are Sadaqa, Zakat, and Waqf. This is called the "hierarchy of Islamic charitable spending" or "hierarchy of Fisabillah spending". The Islamic proposition is Waqf for health, education, and water assets—which can be categorized as social infrastructure. These sectors should be part of concessional financing (Qarz Hasan)—but not grants. People can allocate some part of their wealth to funds for investment and with the returns develop Waqf assets for the health, education, and water sectors. There is a general tendency to propose Zakat, which is a grant, for social infrastructure development; however, Waqf is the business model for social infrastructure development in Islam. Zakat should be distributed directly to the poor. Withholding Zakat with the pretext of any form of investment for the poor or development of social infrastructure is not acceptable in Islam (Gundogdu, 2019b).

The traditional approach for categorizing infrastructure is presented in Box 6.1. Here, unlike in the Islamic approach, economic and social infrastructures are mingled. According to the understanding of economics in Islam, social infrastructure—health, education, and water—is subject to the Waqf business model, while economic infrastructures should be the domain of the private sector (Diallo & Gundogdu, 2021) (Table 6.1).

There is neither a universal definition nor a universal classification/categorization of infrastructure (Baskakova & Malafeev, 2017; Torrisi, 2009). Baskakova and Malafeev (2017), expanding the work of Torrisi (2009), provide a comparative analysis of the approaches to infrastructure classification: Hansen (1965) comes closest to the Islamic reflection of infrastructure by categorizing infrastructure as two aspects:

Table 6.1 Infrastructure categorization

1. **Energy**, which is broken down into the following subsectors: electricity generation, electricity transmission or distribution, natural gas (including gas flaring), energy efficiency, and district heating or cooling
2. **Water, sewage, and sanitation**, which is broken down into the following subsectors: water (including supply, treatment, transportation, and distribution), sewage, wastewater treatment, and irrigation
3. **Municipal solid waste (MSW)**, which is broken down into the following subsectors: collection and transport, treatment and disposal, and integrated MSW
4. **Social infrastructure**, which is broken down into the following subsectors: health care, education, and public facilities
5. **Transport**, which is broken down into the following subsectors: airports, ports, railways, mass transit, roads, and inland waterways
6. **Information and communications technology (ICT)**

Source Operating Guidelines of Global Infrastructure Facility, World Bank (2019)

1. Economic infrastructure
2. Social infrastructure.

This classification is not perfectly aligned with Islamic methodology as it includes irrigation under economic infrastructure and public order and law under social infrastructure. Islamic classification is based more on a business model for service provision. The infrastructure that requires community ownership is classified under social infrastructure. The infrastructure that necessitates private service provision is classified under economic infrastructure. Public order and law necessitate state provision of services. Hence, investment for such asset development should be done by states. Islam proposes community ownership for health, education, and water sector assets, while encouraging private service provision in transport, energy, and ICT sectors, which does not necessarily mean big economic infrastructure assets. Islamic preferences are against monopolies as much as possible—and if impossible, counterbalancing policies to avoid exploitation of dominant positions by big corporations. It is all about sustainability: in Islam infrastructure can be classified based on service provision to ensure sustainability. In relation to sustainability and classifications, infrastructure can be defined as follows:

> Infrastructures are enablers for the sustainable functioning and progress of society.

The term "enablers" is used instead of "assets" because technological development may make big assets redundant and provide an enabling environment with small and flexible tangible and intangible structures. For example, a wire was required to provide communication a century ago. The communication enablers have moved on from this tangible asset to intangible systems. Besides, project assets in a state of rack and ruin should not be defined as infrastructure as they would deter the functioning of society. Instead, such assets should be defined as a burden if sustainability is not ensured. Therefore, the main defining parameter for infrastructure is being an enabler, either tangible or intangible, and being sustainable.

Table 6.2 summarizes the Islamic categorization of infrastructure. Public order and law-related infrastructures are not included under social infrastructure as they come under the direct responsibility of state authorities.

Unlike the conventional approach, the water sector should not be commodified in Islam as water has been the subject of Waqf—and hence

Table 6.2 Infrastructure subsectors

	Sector	Subsector
Economic infrastructure (Private Sector Provides Services)	Transport	Airports, ports, railways, mass transit, and roads
	ICT	First mile
	Energy	Electricity generation, electricity transmission and distribution, natural gas, energy efficiency, and district heating and cooling
Social infrastructure (Community Waqf Provides Services)	Solid waste	Collection and transport, integrated municipal solid waste, and treatment disposal
	Water	Water supply (supply of potable water and agricultural irrigation including water treatment, transport, and distribution), sewage, wastewater treatment, and drainage for irrigation
	Health	Primary, secondary, and tertiary health care
	Education	Primary, secondary, and tertiary education

Source Author

fits into the health and education sector. The water sector's position as part of social infrastructure is clear. On the other hand, the solid waste issue has not been presented in the early times of Islam. It is placed under social infrastructure as it has characteristics of both sewage and wastewater treatment. Both the waste sector (clean water supply, sewage, and solid wastewater treatment) and solid waste are key components of the health sector. The provision of these two infrastructure sector services substantially enhances public health. Hence, both the water sector and the solid waste sector should be part of social infrastructure given their strong interlinkage with public health (Andres et al., 2015). Irrigation and drainage is part of rural development. It is placed under the water sector as part of social infrastructure because of the common watershed shared by communities and the need for community ownership to ensure the sustainability of water resources in specific watershed areas (Diallo & Gundogdu, 2021).

Sustainability Parameters

The Islamic proposition is to ensure everyone in the community has reasonable access to social infrastructure services. No one should be left behind. The provision of social infrastructure is key to guaranteeing equality of opportunities. Present practices mean that only the rich are able to access quality health care and education; however, these should be accessible to youngsters of unfortunate families to ensure opportunities for everyone. The weak social mobility has much to do with the commodification of social infrastructure, and it is totally unacceptable in Islam. On the other hand, private entrepreneurship is much valued and sacred in Islam, as long as they do not inhibit opportunities for others and risk and reward are distributed fairly (Gundogdu, 2019a). This balanced approach to private service provision suggests that, even for economic infrastructure, the best solution is to have a small and flexible infrastructure as much as possible. This is because market structure matters in service pricing and head-to-head competition is the best equitable alternative. In this regard, the technological trend in the energy sector enables SME involvement, and at the same time avoids household tariffing. If big investment is needed, it can be done with minimum burden on the public. In the transport and ICT sectors, the technological trend does not allow small and flexible infrastructure, yet. Although the transport and ICT sectors have similar attributes, they are still considered separate categories because of the following reasons.

First of all, the moral hazard with governments, commercial banks, and project undertakers, including adverse selection in project prioritization, enforces that infrastructure investment should be done, as stated, via specialized multilateral development banks. It is key to identify the right business model to deliver the provision of services based on categorization to avoid moral hazard, adverse selection, and unfairness. The business model in the provision of infrastructure services is key for quality: the infrastructure gap is not the sole problem. For example, having water does not guarantee health, as long as there is no safe and reliable flow. In a similar fashion, being connected to the electricity grid does not ensure the supply of a reliable and continuous current (Fay et al., 2019). The categorization of infrastructure suggests that there is no one-size-fits-all approach. The distinction between economic and social infrastructure brings forth the first sustainability parameter: a business model for service delivery—which means Waqf for social infrastructure and private entrepreneurship for economic infrastructure. The selection of a business model would narrow down options for several Islamic finance contracts to develop assets. The reason there are several contracts, not one cash-lending contract, is to ensure fairness based on the realities of the deal in relation to sustainability (Diallo & Gundogdu, 2021). Therefore, the second parameter is a contract for asset development. The financing contracts would determine the most suitable harnessed resource mobilization methods. The avoidance of tax collection and unwelcome deposit-collecting banking business model defines resource mobilization as a third parameter. The use of public sources and schemes to create an enabling environment for big corporations and the wealthy is not a fair approach to infrastructure development. Hence, it is not sustainable. The issue of resource mobilization becomes more important under such restrictions, particularly because the infrastructure gap to provide very basic services such as electricity, clean drinking water, and sanitation is large (Rozenberg & Fay, 2019).[2] For these three sustainability parameters, we can seek the Islamic best alternatives to ensure the sustainability of infrastructure investment by MDBs. The three parameters are presented in Table 6.3.

The parameters could be expanded; however, as they are, they are concise and comprehensive for MDBs to have sustainable infrastructure investment. Public infrastructure is not included in Table 6.3 because Hisbah, courts, and regulatory and supervisory agencies need to be state-owned in Islam. The question of how to find resources to finance these assets and organizations can be addressed by resource-financed infrastructure (RFI). States have resources other than taxes available to them. For instance, sizable infrastructures of power plants, roads, railways, ICT projects, schools, water projects, and hospitals are financed through RFI (Halland et al., 2014). Unlike Islamic propositions, RFI has been used to develop both economic and social infrastructure. The term "Angola-mode" is used to define this approach, and the long-term results will be observed in due course. Many developing countries, particularly sub-Saharan African, use their natural resources as collateral to access hard currencies. Relatively advanced countries use the receipts from natural

---

[2] Several studies have been done that show the magnitude of the infrastructure gap. Rozenberg and Fay (2019) have highlighted the following: 1 billion people live 2 km from a proper road, 1.2 billion people are without electricity, 663 million people lack access to healthy drinking water, and 2.4 billion people lack proper sanitation facilities.

Table 6.3 Sustainability parameters

	Sector	The business model for service delivery	Contract for asset development	Resource mobilization to scale-up
Economic infrastructure (commercially priced investment)	Transport	PPP	Istisna	Asset-backed Sukuk
	ICT	PPP	Murabaha	Crowdfunding (Mudaraba, Two-Step Murabaha)
	Energy	Off-grid renewable asset to be provided by SMEs	Ijara	Crowdfunding (Parallel Ijara)
Social infrastructure (concessional priced investment—Qarz Hasan)	Solid waste, water, health, and education	Waqf	Istisna for Waqf asset development	Cash Waqf/Cash Waqf Sukuk

Source Author

resources to finance their sovereign wealth funds, by which they ensure that the next generations can also benefit from the present exploitation of natural resources. As with tax resources, FRI is also an unfair practice, which works against future generations in particular. Nevertheless, the common practice of RFI suggests that states have capabilities to generate revenue—such as revenue streams from natural resources and fees from regulatory and supervisory services—to develop and sustain public infrastructure. Keeping the ownership of the land with the state and the sale of this right for 99 years can generate enough resources for the government.

BUSINESS MODEL FOR SERVICE DELIVERY

The key to sustainability is to identify the equitable business models by which risk and rewards are distributed fairly. The business model should be able to ensure long-term quality service provision and maintenance of the assets while inhibiting the exploitation of service users. The project assets should be well maintained, resilient to natural hazards, and affordable to consumers in the long term. The business model should fit to impede moral hazard and adverse selection while addressing the maintenance and financial sustainability of services (Diallo & Gundogdu, 2021). The ideal situation is to have a technology that does not necessitate big infrastructure assets. The second best option is to have community ownership. Such community ownership is possible with social infrastructure sectors: education, health, water, and solid waste management at the municipal or county level. Hence, they constitute social infrastructure. In the case of energy, transport, and ICT, the project assets would extend from one region to another. Based on present technology, a community ownership approach would be counterproductive. Islam does not propose community ownership in economic infrastructure either (Gundogdu, 2019c). When technology evolves, there is less need for big infrastructure. For example, prospective progress in levitation technology would make toll roads, ports, and airports less significant.

In the area of economic infrastructure, when technological progress allows big infrastructure to be replaced by small and flexible ones, this does not culminate in community ownership but in small-scaled SMEs or household ownership. Therefore, it is still private ownership even though large corporations' service provision is no longer needed. Accordingly, it might be expected that community ownership for social infrastructure and SME/household ownership for economic infrastructure is expected to shape the future of equitable Islamic infrastructure investment. Until the technological progress creates this opportunity, big companies will continue to play some role in economic infrastructure in particular. Hence, their involvement should be with checks and balances to ensure fairness. It is not only an issue of Islamic abhorrence of tax collection but also maintenance problems that should define a business model for sustainability. With strong inherent asset management and maintenance features, PPPs ensure quality service provision in the long term. PPPs present a strong potential for economic infrastructure. The issue of maintenance suggests that PPP is better for sustainability; however, where there is a household tariffing scheme or social infrastructure, PPP concessions have serious side effects. For instance, default rates are highest in the energy sector (Jobst, 2018).[3] Hence, the most suitable business model

---

[3] The Azure-Edo Power Project in Nigeria and the Azito Power Plant Expansion Project in Cote d'Ivoire—two gas-fired power plant projects—have been developed with novel risk mitigation measures in the PPP structure to overcome failures specific to energy projects. We should observe the outcome of these two projects in order to discern the

for the energy sector appears to be off-grid and/or mini-grid renewable electricity. It is still based on private ownership but without the need for big companies and big infrastructure. The technological trend in renewable energy—solar or wind—favors the provision of energy without transmission lines or without imposing tariffs on households.

Present progress in renewable energy alternatives has already paved the way for small and flexible off-grid or mini-grid alternatives in the energy sector. The issue has been resource mobilization for scaling up. Recent product development for the distributed renewables for energy access (DREA) system introduced a crowdfunding platform to mobilize resources to finance local SMEs for the installation of the system.[4] This is a good example of future trends. It is a small and flexible alternative to the traditional large power systems, with its large production facilities and big networks. The traditional approach needs big networks to reach out to remote areas. The economics of this massive investment inhibits the provision of energy to remote areas. DREA systems can provide electricity for appliances in cooling, heating, cooking, and lighting. It can do so using an off-grid or mini-grid system on a standalone basis without the need for a large distribution network. This can be classified as "variable renewable energy". As the name implies, it is characterized by variability and uncertainty. Such characteristics lead to a technical challenge in the provision of reliable energy in a way that balances supply and demand. The remedy is to develop energy storage systems. Directing huge infrastructure investments from power plants and transmission lines to energy storage systems for off-grid and mini-grid renewable energy would be a much better solution.

As with the household tariffs in the energy sector, the PPP business model for social infrastructure can lead to exploitation in the water, health, and education sectors (Gundogdu, 2019c). Contract cancelation is highest in water-sector PPP projects (Marcelo et al., 2017). The Islamic business model for social infrastructure service provision is community Waqf. PPP yields favorable results in the transport sector (Gundogdu, 2018). Although financing and operating costs are higher with PPP when compared to public investment, these are compensated by savings

---

sustainability dimensions of the PPP business model for the energy sector (details by IFC, 2016, Mitigation Private Infrastructure Project Risks).

[4] The product is developed by Bandar Al Oweis from the Islamic Development Bank.

in asset management and maintenance. Besides, with limited concession time, PPP sponsors to ensure the most efficient project design, including resilient assets against natural hazards as well as innovative and cost-efficient methods of service provision. For instance, a public procurement approach to seaport traffic would be to expand the port, while PPP sponsoring companies would come up with a novel port design and a management information system (MIS) to deliver the same amount of targeted traffic without additional assets. A PPP approach can compensate for some part of perceived infrastructure investment by filling performance gaps in governance and using existing infrastructure more efficiently. For instance, there is no need to keep investing in water supply infrastructure without having completed a water audit to identify inefficiencies, leakage-detection procedures, and necessary repairs to existing systems. Another example would be project design to ensure that project assets need minimum maintenance and can withstand natural hazards. For example, positioning transmission line towers at a safe distance from trees will ensure the power is not disrupted should a tree fall over in a storm, or considering the possibility of flooding in the project design for a wastewater treatment plant would substantially decrease the risk of damage to assets should a flood occur. To sum up, having assets in a state of rack and ruin does not happen if PPP is used, as with the Waqf business model (Diallo & Gundogdu, 2021). Yet it does not mean PPP is a menace for all sectors. PPP works smoothly for ICT first mile and for transport, both of which present similar characteristics (Gundogdu, 2019c). As with transport, ICT infrastructure investment should be done with PPPs. However, the specific characteristics of ICT assets suggest a different financing contract for asset development.

Contracts for Asset Development

The statistics in infrastructure investment indicate that it is the energy sector infrastructure that is most likely to default. The difficulty in tariff collection is an important factor if such risks are not transferred with off-take contracts to mitigate contingencies from price and demand uncertainty. However, having a suitable business model to address such default risk is not enough on its own as a general principle for infrastructure investment. There exists an incremental default risk during the "greenfield" stage (construction phase), and the grading of an infrastructure investment substantially converges to investment grade at "brownfield" stage once the project assets are fully operational (Jobst, 2018). That is, the default risk profile is hump-shaped. Identifying a proper contract in asset development is key to mitigating the default risk in the greenfield stage. Besides, based on the characteristics of the sector asset, development contracts should ensure the fair distribution of rights, obligations, and responsibilities of parties. Both transport and ICT sectors can better be subject of PPP business model, yet project assets would require different contracts. In the case of transport projects, environmental and social safeguard (ESS) is key, and financiers should not shun their long-term responsibilities. The effect of project assets on the environment and communities should be factored into the investment decision. The project design should include ESS. The negative consequences of project development on communities are not technically insurable. For instance, damage caused by road construction on orchids around would not be covered under insurance policies; as such, the consequence is predictable and can be taken into account by the project developer. Istisna contracts put the burden on financiers for any environmental and social disasters caused by the project even after project completion. Islamic finance contracts encourage more merit-based employment of bankers who can tackle such complexities. Excessive use of insurance would lead to moral hazard in project investment. It is not only traditional political risk insurance but more the new methods and means that shape the risk mitigation map of insurance for infrastructure investment. Surety Bond Insurance, which guarantees the completion of a project in the event of financial default, is a good example. The proposal for use of insurance against climate change risks, such as drought, is another example of excessive use of insurance policies that would lead to moral hazard by financial institutions against the public. In a similar fashion, the multilateral development banks' (MDBs') A Loan/B Loan mechanism, by which MDBs inflict first loss, is another example of a risk mitigation mechanism that leads to moral hazard. PPP laws covering project completion risk by the government is another example of the new methods that diminish the role and risk of financial institutions in project finance. The Istisna contract of Islamic finance, however, makes the financial institution the main actor in project development. Shari'ah restriction would not allow the chunk of such risk mitigation methods in an Istisna contract.

Political risk insurance is a standard part of the risk management package: breach of contract (BoC) and indirect expropriations of businesses belonging to multinational corporations are widespread. There are reasons for local government to breach the contract. First, new country leadership may discern irregularities in the deal done by predecessors in which they are not part of the deal for the concession given to multinational corporations. Second, in the case of natural resource concessions, host countries may have a strong incentive to breach the contract during a commodity price boom. Besides, the probability of contract breach increases as a project matures and after large global shocks such as natural disasters, particularly in politically instable and undemocratic countries (Nose, 2014). The presence of MDBs, in the form of participation in lending, equity contribution, and insurance of financial guarantee products, in PPP deals substantially decreases the probability of expropriations (Marcelo & House, 2016). Perhaps it is because the host country is the shareholder of the specific MDB undertaking any obligatory role in the project.

For all these risk issues, an MDB's involvement with PPP would work for the transport sector in particular (Gundogdu, 2019c). The best fitting Islamic finance contract, with fair distribution of rights and obligations, is Istisna for PPP transport projects. On the other hand, the case of ICT first mile is different. The importance of first-mile assets for the whole economy deters lien on project assets. Case Box 6.2 presents the case of a submarine cable project.

Case Box 6.2: The SEA-ME-WE-4 submarine fiber-optic cable, Bangladesh

People across the world want to be connected—to information, to markets, to each other. In these recent years, being connected has increasingly come to mean two things: mobile phones and the Internet. Faster internet and better mobile connections provide a host of benefits. Traders can contact their suppliers to find out market prices; families can communicate quickly and cheaply across the globe; while students and professionals have access to a range of digitized information that was once unimaginable. In order to take advantage of these opportunities, connection speeds need to be fast enough to cope with the pace of modern life. And in the early years of the twenty-first century, Bangladesh was lagging behind the rest of South Asia.

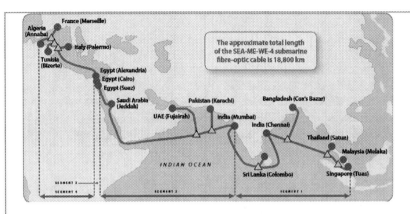

Location of the SEA-ME-WE-4 submarine fibre-optic cable.

The SEA-ME-WE-4 submarine fibre-optic cable: The project began in 2005 and was completed in 2008. The Islamic Development Bank (IsDB) provided US$ 60 million, with the Government of Bangladesh contributing the remaining US$ 8.02 million. This covered the cost of 1,065 km of cable, which was installed by the international submarine cable consortium South East Asia (SEA)–Middle East (ME)–Western Europe (WE), along with technical partners Alcatel Lucent of France and Fujitsu of Japan. The SEAME-WE-4 submarine fiber-optic cable already served thirteen other countries, from France in Europe, via Saudi Arabia in the Middle East, to Singapore in South-East Asia; it now connects to Bangladesh at Cox's Bazar, in the south-east of the country. The project also covered the costs of implementation and testing equipment and facilities. Bangladesh became a member of the SEA-ME-WE-4 Consortium through the Bangladesh Submarine Cable Company Limited (BSCCL).

Source Islamic Development Bank.

In the Bangladesh submarine project, cables were provided with Murabaha sale. The government contribution was confined to civil work; it is standard practice in MDBs infrastructure investment for government to contribute a portion of the investment amount. BSCCL is a government-owned company. Although a government would be able to control the service provision and pricing, in the long-run government ownership in service quality and asset maintenance prove to be inferior to private sector concessions. Had this project been done with PPP, a project company would have contributed to the portion of the investment amount instead of the government.

The major problem with Murabaha sale is resource mobilization. Since the ownership of the items financed transfers to the loan seeker, there is no way to develop asset-backed securitization. In a Murabaha sale, there is no way of having securitized assets that can be traded in financial markets in the secondary market, particularly Sukuk. Establishing a lien such as in the form of Ijara—which would allow securitization of proceeds and secondary market trading—on ICT assets such as fiber optics is very problematic. In the event of a dispute between the financiers and the project company, any lien action on the assets would disrupt the whole country. Hence, it is more suitable to transfer ownership of assets to a project sponsor with a Murabaha sale. Unlike with ICT first mile, as a general principle, it is better to develop project assets with an Istisna contract, which fairly distributes the risk, rewards, and obligations, especially in cases where heavy civil work is involved, as with transportation projects. Istisna contracts should also be used for Waqf asset development in the provision of social infrastructures.

In the energy sector, distributed renewables for energy access (DREA) systems require Ijara contracts to provide necessary assets to households through SMEs. Unlike with ICT, financiers can have a lien on Ijara assets. It is important to avoid any risk mitigation mechanism of group collateral practice of microfinance: it is unfair. The Ijara contract with a lien on assets would allow securitization for trade in the secondary market—that is, assuming there is no restriction on the assignment of lease receipts under local jurisdiction. Note that such restrictions are there in many countries for deposit-collecting commercial banks. A more creative resource mobilization method should be employed for the energy sector. Financing the asset installation and mobilizing the resources for such programs should be harnessed for scale-up; this is key for the success of these new methods. The next section provides the details of the provision of assets with Ijara through SMEs vis-à-vis crowdfunding resource mobilization for the energy sector as an alternative to recourse to deposit collecting banks' balance sheets. Before going into details of resource mobilization, the case of infrastructure investment clearly shows us that each Islamic finance contract has a unique characteristic to serve based on the realities on the ground. Unlike organized Tawarruq, aka commodity Murabaha, and conventional loans—both are cash lending—Islamic finance proposes unique financing contracts to ensure fairness and, thus, sustainability based on the specification of the deal. The same holds for the resource mobilization proposition of Islamic finance. There is no one-size-fits-all resource mobilization contract or method in Islamic finance.

Resource Mobilization to Scale-up

Infrastructure investment as a percentage of output—for which the stock of public capital spending is usually taken as a proxy—has been declining since 1990, particularly in developing countries (Jobst, 2018). These countries need to invest around 6.1% of their GDP in order to maintain service levels of existing assets and fulfill additional infrastructure demand (Ruiz-Núñer & Wei, 2015). Financing is key to achieve a sustainable and thriving society. However, if it is used improperly, it will destroy not only the economy but also society. Financial contracts and resource mobilization conduits should ensure that there is no unfair wealth transfer from one segment of society to another. For example, resorting to tax resources is a wealth transfer from the poor to those benefiting from infrastructure investment. To avoid using tax resources, recourse to alternative resource mobilization tools is an important element of sustainability in infrastructure investment. The same holds for tapping into deposits of deposit-collecting banks. Deposit-collecting banking is not a viable business model to underpin Islamic finance (Diallo & Gundogdu, 2021). This means neither tax resources nor deposit banking would provide a sustainable solution to mobilize resources for infrastructure investment. Even so, most of developing countries are not able to address the infrastructure gap owing to insufficient domestic savings and a lack of sufficient fiscal space (Schwartz et al., 2014). Hence, tax resources and savings in deposit banks for infrastructure development are neither advisable nor available in a sufficient manner to address the infrastructure gap. Indeed, decades of resource mobilization for infrastructure investment approximated conventional thinking to Islamic wisdom: crowding-in private capital is proposed as a paradigm shift in development finance. Prolonged low-interest rates in developed countries and infrastructure investment returns with long-term fixed-income features fit well with the needs of insurance companies (Jobst, 2018). Other institutional investors would be pension funds and sovereign wealth funds. This convergence is more of a fact for mobilizing resources for economic infrastructure.

Given the peculiarities of Islamic finance for asset development and its link with resource mobilization mechanisms, the following Islamic alternatives can fill the bill: asset-backed Sukuk for transport PPP, two-step

Murabaha and Mudaraba for ICT, crowdfunding for SME Ijara financing for the energy sector, Cash Waqf Fund, and Cash Waqf Sukuk for Waqf asset development for social infrastructure. Figure 6.1 illustrates the case of crowdfunding for the energy sector.

1. The mandated development bank and Solar Partner (SP), a local SME, sign "parallel Ijara" agreements. The mandated development bank holds an e-wallet account in an accredited payment institution.
2. The Crowdfunding Company (CC) and the mandated development bank signed an "agency" agreement. To manage and administer the financing facility for a fee, the bank appoints CC.
3. It is CC's responsibility to check for conditions precedent to disbursement before disbursement request from SP based on the agreement.
4. The mandated development bank sends its portion of the fund to CC following a request from CC, which makes direct disbursement to the manufacturer of SHS (supplier) after adding funds from the crowdfunding participants.

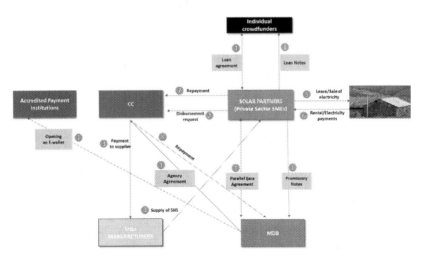

Fig. 6.1 Unlocking energy access finance through crowdfunding (*Source* Diallo and Gundogdu [2021])

5. The supplier delivers the SHS to SP after the exchange of form of offer and acceptance.
6. SP installs the SHS after signing a lease agreement with the lessee, the end beneficiary.
7. CC receives Ijara receipts through SP which collects receipts from the end beneficiaries.
8. Based on the predetermined agreement, the crowdfunding participants receive funds from CC.

Because the energy sector is an economic infrastructure, resources should be mobilized with commercially market-financing prices. The same is the case for ICT. However, unlike Ijara, the use of Murabaha sale in the provision of project assets would entail the employment of two-step Murabaha and Mudaraba resource mobilization contracts for ICT. However, these contracts would cause a major bottleneck because they are asset-based. Hence, there is no way for secondary market trading owing to Shari'ah constraints. Secondary market trading provides liquidity management opportunities for Islamic banks. Unlike these asset-based contracts, PPP can provide such an opportunity. The assets of transport PPPs can be the subject of tradable, asset-backed Sukuk. Asset-backed transport PPPs would enable a secondary market, and hence would be an excellent liquidity management tool for Islamic financial institutions (Gundogdu, 2019c).

Cash Waqf Fund and Cash Waqf Sukuk are contemporary resource mobilization tools for Waqf Development. Unlike economic infrastructure contracts, contracts for social infrastructure should not be commodified. For the transport, ICT, and energy sectors, resources should be mobilized from the market with commercially priced resources. For social infrastructure in developing Waqf assets with Istisna, resources should be mobilized via concessional loans (Qarz Hasan). Cash Waqf Fund can mobilize resources via Cash Waqf Sukuk. And, with resources received, Cash Waqf Fund can continue the development of further assets (Gundogdu, 2018). Note that Cash Waqf Sukuk is not a commercially priced instrument; it just gives easy access for philanthropists to allocate some part of their wealth to Waqh on a temporary basis and deduct it from their Zakat(able) wealth. Zakat resources cannot be used for social infrastructure development as they should be distributed directly to the needy. Nevertheless, allocating some part of Zakat(able) amount to Cash

Waqf for social infrastructure can be a part of Fi'sabilillah spending, yet it cannot count toward a Zakat obligation (Gundogdu, 2019b).

The major difference between Islamic and conventional infrastructure investment relates to categorization. Islamic economics clearly delineates social infrastructure from economic infrastructure. Market structure, price regulation issues, and asset ownership for the infrastructure define the Islamic approach. As Islamic infrastructure investment suggests, economic infrastructure should ensure fairness to all stakeholders including banks, project companies, the government, and the community. In an ideal case, there would be no need for economic infrastructure or small and flexible assets so long as technological progress allows. Until then, the presence of big corporations should be counter-balanced with anti-monopoly measures to avoid exploitation of the public and an excessive burden on the government. A regulated natural monopoly is an option where a regulatory body sets service prices. Either way, economic infrastructure should definitely be provided by the private sector because it would perform better in maintaining the project assets, designing the project for resilient infrastructure, and managing the finances of the project assets. Infrastructure assets, including airports, roads, water systems, transmission lines, and power plants, are vulnerable to natural perils. Therefore, a resilience feature should be part of the project design. These are the key components of avoiding infrastructure directly developed by the government that is in a state of rack and ruin. The Islamic and conventional approaches are similar in that they both propose using private entrepreneurship for economic infrastructure. Avoiding big corporations and providing these services with small and flexible infrastructure is the rationale that should apply. In a similar fashion, the ideal case is to use technology that does not require infrastructure. For example, transportation should focus on levitation technologies to dismiss the need for roads and ports. In the energy sector, instead of having large centralized energy production assets and massive distribution networks, it would be better to focus on off-grid and mini-grid energy kits, particularly in energy storage systems for renewable energy. If infrastructure investments direct resources away from big transport and energy projects to levitation technology and renewable energy technologies, then we will probably have technology that does not require such massive infrastructures sooner than expected. This would also sort out the adverse selection and moral hazard embedded in project appraisal and the prioritization process, which has proved to be rather informal even with the use of IPFs by public authorities. If there is no need for an infrastructure investment decision, there is little, if any, an opportunity for corruption.

As for social infrastructure, what is right in economic infrastructure, of necessity for private sector involvement, is wrong for social infrastructure. Unlike economic infrastructure, the Islamic approach totally differs from the conventional one. The focus of the conventional approach is the availability of social infrastructure, while in the Islamic approach it is inclusiveness: no one should be left behind when it comes to ensuring equality of opportunities in society. Safe water should be not only available but also affordable for all. Besides, the focus of social infrastructure investment should be the primary services, such as primary education and primary health services. For instance, investment in higher education would transfer resources to the middle and upper-middle class at the expense of the poor. In a similar fashion, focusing on specialized oncology clinics would transfer resources from youngsters to the elderly. Consideration of such segment preferences to avoid unfairness to some parts of society would be a wise move for infrastructure investment.

What makes the Islamic approach unique is its propositions for social infrastructure. Social infrastructure should be provided with Waqf in Islam in order to avoid the commodification of health, education, water, and solid waste. Private sector involvement in social infrastructure leads to inefficient social services and unfair excessive prices (Diallo & Gundogdu, 2021). Resources for social infrastructure development should be mobilized with Qarz Hasan in Cash Waqf Fund and Cash Waqf Sukuk, but not from Zakat. The idea of using Zakat to constitute a fund to develop social infrastructure is utterly unacceptable, as Zakat should directly be distributed from the wealthy to the needy. Islamic economics instead proposes Qarz Hasan and Waqf business models for social infrastructure investment. From an Islamic economics point of view, what is perfectly correct of private sector involvement for economic infrastructure investment is perfectly incorrect for social infrastructure investment as Islam observes equitability. The wisdom derived from Islamic economics and finance provides fitting business models, financing contracts, and resource mobilization methods to develop infrastructure that enables the functioning of society in a sustainable manner to progress. Food security, affordable housing, and poverty alleviation can only be achieved with enabling infrastructure. The present way of infrastructure development undermines food security, affordable housing, and poverty alleviation efforts.

References

Acemoglu, D. (2005). Politics and economics in weak and strong states. *Journal of Monetary Economics, 52,* 1199–1226.

Andres, L., Biller, D., & Dappe, M. H. (2015). *A methodological framework for prioritizing infrastructure investment* (Policy Research Working Paper 7433). World Bank.

Baskakova, I. V., & Malafeev, N. S. (2017). The concept of infrastructure: Definition, classification and methodology for empirical evaluation. *Economic Theory, 3*(71), 29–41.

Braese, J., Rentschler, J., & Hallgatte, S. (2019). *Resilient infrastructure for thriving firms: A review of the evidence* (Policy Research Working Paper 8895). World Bank.

Calderon, C., & Serven, L. (2014). *Infrastructure, growth, and inequality: An overview* (Policy Research Working Paper 7034). World Bank.

Chatterjee, S., & Turnovsky, S. J. (2012). Infrastructure and inequality. *European Economic Review, 56,* 1730–1745.

Choi, J., Fukase, E., & Zeufack, A. (2019). *Global Value Chain (GVC) participation, competition, and markup: Firm-level evidence from Ethiopia* (Background paper). World Bank.

Diallo, A. T., & Gundogdu, A. S. (2021). *Islamic finance, sustainable development, and infrastructure projects.* Palgrave Macmillan.

Esfahani, H. S., & Ramírez, M. T. (2003). Institutions, infrastructure, and economic growth. *Journal of Development Economics, 70*(2), 443–477.

Fay, M., Han, S., Lee, H. I., Mastruzzi, M., & Cho, M. (2019). *Hitting the trillion mark: A look at how much countries are spending on infrastructure* (Policy Research Working Paper 8730). World Bank.

Gundogdu, A. S. (2018). An inquiry into Islamic finance from the perspective of sustainable development goals. *European Journal of Sustainable Development, 7*(4), 381–390.

Gundogdu, A. S. (2019a). *A modern perspective of Islamic economics and finance.* Emerald Publishing Limited.

Gundogdu, A. S. (2019b). Poverty, hunger and inequality in the context of Zakat and Waqf. *Darulfunun Ilahiyat, 30*(1), 49–64.

Gundogdu, A. S. (2019c). Determinants of success in Islamic public–private partnership projects (PPPs) in the context of SDGs. *Turkish Journal of Islamic Economics, 6*(2), 25–43.

Haider, S. Z., Amjad, M. U., Ullah, S., & Naveed, T. A. (2012). Role of infrastructure in economic growth: A case study of Pakistan. *Journal of Asian Development Studies, 1*(1), 13–21.

Halland, H., Beardsworth, J., Land, B., & Schmidt, J. (2014). *Resource financed infrastructure: A discussion on a new form of infrastructure financing.* World Bank.

Hansen, N. M. (1965). The structure and determinants of local public investment expenditures. *Review of Economics and Statistics, 2,* 150–162.

Jobst, A. A. (2018). *Credit risk dynamics of infrastructure investment* (Policy Research Working Paper 8373). World Bank.

Khandker, S. R., Samad, H. A., Ali, R., & Barnes, D. F. (2014). Who benefits most from rural electrification? Evidence in India. *The Energy Journal, 35*(2).

Kornejew, M., Rentschler, J., & Hallagatte, S. (2019). *Well spent: How government determines the effectiveness of infrastructure investment* (Policy Research Working Paper 8894). World Bank.

Luo, X., & Xu, X. (2018). *Infrastructure, value chains, and economic upgrade* (Policy Research Working Paper 8547). World Bank.

Marcelo, D., & House, S. (2016). *Effect of multilateral support on infrastructure PPP contract cancellation* (Policy Research Working Paper 7751). World Bank.

Marcelo, D., House, S., Mandri-Perrott, C., & Schwartz, J. (2017). *Do countries learn from experience in infrastructure PPP: PPP practice and contract cancellation* (Policy Research Working Paper 8054). World Bank.

Marcelo, D., Mandri-Perrott, C., House, S., & Schwartz, J. (2016). *Prioritizing infrastructure investment; a framework for government decision making* (Policy Research Working Paper 7674). World Bank.

Nose, M. (2014, January). *Triggers of contract breach: Contract design, shocks, or institutions?* (World Bank Policy Research Working Paper No. 6738). SSRN: https://ssrn.com/abstract=2375457

Petrie, M. (2010). *Promoting public investment efficiency: A synthesis of country experiences.* Paper presented at World Bank Preparatory Workshop, Promoting Public Investment Efficiency, Global Lessons and Resources of Strengthening World Bank Support for Client Countries.

Porter, M. E. (2000). Location, competition, and economic development: Local clusters in a global economy. *Economic Development Quarterly, 14*(1), 15–34.

Rozenberg, J., & Fay, M. (2019). *Beyond the gap: How countries can afford the infrastructure they need while protecting the planet.* Sustainable Infrastructure. World Bank. https://openknowledge.worldbank.org/handle/10986/31291

Ruiz-Núñez, F., & Wei, Z. (2015, September 17). *Infrastructure investment demands in emerging markets and developing economies* (World Bank Working Paper Series No. 7414). World Bank Group.

Sanchez-Robles, B. (1998). Infrastructure investment and growth: Some empirical evidence. *Contemporary Economic Policy, 16*(1), 98–108.

Schwartz, J. Z., Ruiz-Núñez, F., & Chelsky, J. (2014, March 20–21). Closing the infrastructure finance gap: Addressing risk. In A. Heath & R. Matthew (Eds.), *Financial flows and infrastructure financing: Conference Proceedings.* Reserve Bank of Australia. www.rba.gov.au/publications/confs/2014/pdf/conf-vol-2014.pdf

Shihata, I. (2000). *The World Bank inspection panel: In practice*. Oxford University Press.

Timilisina, G., Hochman, G., & Song, Z. (2020). *Infrastructure, economic growth, and poverty: A review* (Policy Research Working Paper 9258). World Bank.

Torrisi, G. (2009). *Public infrastructure: Definition, classification and measurement issues* (MPRA Paper 12990). University Library of Munich, Germany.

Woetzel, J., & Pohl, H. (2014). *Infrastructure: Doing more with less* (Policy Research Working Paper 6882). World Bank.

World Bank. (2019). *World development report 2020: Trading for development in the age of global value chains' (English)*. World Bank Group.

CHAPTER 7

The Role of the State

To-dos and not-to-dos of the sovereign states to assure food security, and affordable housing, hence, poverty alleviation.

The state's role from an Islamic perspective should be limited to regulation, supervision, and law enforcement rather than direct lending or construction of housing, infrastructure, or agricultural production. The state should provide an enabling environment for society to overcome its challenges. The state should also not directly assist poor people from the public budget but develop and manage a safety net structure with Zakat for direct wealth transfer from the rich to the poor.

The finance can be used to create an enabling environment for all. It should not be structured in a way that enriches selfish individuals. Conventional economics and finance are based on the faith that selfishness and greed are good. Adam Smith, founder of modern economics, in his book in the name of "*The Theory of Moral Sentiments*," tried to convince his readers with the eloquence of poetry: "we are not ready to suspect any person of being defective in selfishness." Milton Friedman championed greed and selfishness for human achievement. Their utopia of so-called rational thinking and selfish and greedy people gave rise to self-destructive wars and financial crises. Once everybody in society gets infected with greed and selfishness and becomes a so-called rational thinker, the game theory predicts stalemate or irreversible destruction. One thing that Milton Friedman was right about is that both capitalism and communism run on greed to control. Both of them are cynical.

© The Author(s), under exclusive license to Springer Nature Switzerland AG 2023
A. S. Gundogdu, *Food Security, Affordable Housing, and Poverty*, Palgrave Studies in Islamic Banking, Finance, and Economics, https://doi.org/10.1007/978-3-031-27689-7_7

Like other traditional world religions, the Islamic approach abhors greed and selfishness. It discourages hoarding to provide space for all members of society in a way not to create financial sustainability worries for individuals, both the rich and the poor. Islam encourages spending on family and charitable spending for the community. The wisdom gets much clearer after the "Greed is good" philosophy has led the world into chaos many times with financial crises and wars. We can reach Pareto optimum point by agreeing on certain ethical principles but not the self-destructing concept of selfishness. And this is only achievable with *iman* (faith). The subject of finance should be tough to create value for society but not deceive people into a zero-sum game. In a situation where all knows the game's rule, people are stuck in a stalemate and cannot reach a Pareto optimal level that is better for all. To achieve Pareto optimum point, we should agree on specific Islamic rules to avoid self-destruction in game theory.

The states in both communist and capitalist systems turned out to assume arbitrary roles to address the imperfections their ideologies precipitated. In today's world, the state's role is arbitrary regardless of wisdom to confine the role of the state to law enforcement and regulating and supervising the markets. The issue is particularly acute in the financial sector: bankers convinced the states about their capacity to manage their risks and deliver the financial result. They end up bailed out or provided capital injection at the expense of households. They can implement the notion of greed and selfishness until the public realizes that this is not in their best interest. It is not the state's responsibility to save financial institutions, which happens in capitalism, or produce consumer products, which happens in communism. The Islamic perspective defines the role of the state within Hisbah.

Hisbah[1]

Hisbah, which is known to have emerged in the period of Muhammad (ﷺ) and is an institution-specific to Islam, is an organization established to live in a way that the Islamic principles are followed in every aspect of life. Even if the duties undertaken by such an institution differ in each period,

---

[1] Based on MA thesis of Mahmut Dost under the supervision of the author. "A comparison of Medina Rules with the Ottoman State Practice vis-à-vis Hisbe Organization", 2021.

it has undertaken many essential duties while preserving the reason for its emergence. The first application of Hisbah, which is a natural institution created by Muhammad (ﷺ). Evidence of Hisbah, which means enjoining good and forbidding evil, is mentioned in Quran.

> Let there be a group among you who call ⌐others¬ to goodness, encourage what is good, and forbid what is evil—it is they who will be successful. (3:104)

Muhammad (ﷺ)'s efforts to do good and destroy evil covered all areas of life. But later, when his responsibilities increased, he appointed some suitably qualified people under the name of *Sahibu's Suk* to inspect tradespeople and artisans. Muhammed (ﷺ) appointed some female *Sahibu's Suk* as well. Hisbah developed into an entire fledge government organization throughout the history of Islamic states (Kallek, 1998: 135). Its role was confined to law enforcement, regulation, and supervision of markets. The things the state should and should not do are clearly defined.

INFRASTRUCTURE: OUTPUT, OUTCOME, AND SERVICES

Reflections so far suggest that states have an important role in the economy: regulating and supervising land use policy and assuring that Zakat is adequately paid. The states shall keep playing an important role in human societies. Still, it should be transformed from a tax collecting and rent distributing role, which is the case as-is, into assuring the sustainable and affordable provision of infrastructure services reasonably. In this regard, it is key to defining infrastructure services and the role of government. To stimulate progress, it is crucial to define the outcome vs. output. For instance, the outcome of giving a public-private partnership (PPP) concession for a seaport is to guarantee effective transport service. The same outcome can be achieved via prospective levitation technologies, making railways, roads, and sea ports non-relevant. So what matters here is the provision of services. The role of government should be defined within infrastructure service provision. Islamic wisdom advises private service provision for economic infrastructure and Waqf business model for social infrastructure. The role of government is to ensure accountability as defined based on Hisbah. Indeed, the major failure of states throughout history is because they failed to ensure accountability and be involved in economic and social infrastructure services (Gundogdu, 2019).

Table 7.1 shows the role of government in the provision of services. Although historically, neither capitalism nor communism reached their ultimate utopia: which would lead to the collapse of the society and the state anyway: capitalist ideology prefers private service providers, while communist ideology seeks a public service provider business model. Islamic thinking seeks to address each sector's needs based on their realities to assure sustainability and fairness. Hence, economic infrastructure services should be provided by the private sector; social infrastructure services should be provided by the Waqf owned by the community, which uses these services. The role of the state is to assure accountability via Ḥisbah. In Islamic understanding, the government should regulate and supervise the private sector, individuals, and Waqf. It should not provide economic or social infrastructure services. The role of public, private, and community-owned Waqf is listed in Table 7.2.

The table on the role of government can be used to define the states by their ideologies. It would be challenging to see many countries that claim to be Islamic are closer to capitalism or communism than Islam. A country that provides health and education services via the private sector is capitalist, and a country that gives transport, ICT, and energy services can be deemed socialist or communist. An Islamic state would delegate transport, ICT, and energy service provisions to the private sector, and

Table 7.1 Infrastructure sectors

Economic infrastructure	Airports, ports, railways, mass transit, and roads
	ICT first mile
	Electricity generation, electricity transmission, and distribution, natural gas, energy efficiency, and district heating and cooling
Social infrastructure	Solid waste collection and transport, integrated municipal solid waste, and treatment disposal
	Water supply (supply of potable water and agricultural irrigation including water treatment, transport, and distribution), sewage, wastewater treatment, and drainage for irrigation
	Primary, secondary, and tertiary health care
	Primary, secondary, and tertiary education
Accountability infrastructure	Law enforcement, courts, prisons, and regulatory and supervisory agencies

Source Author

Table 7.2 The role of government in Islam

Economic infrastructure	Transport, ICT, and energy	Private service provider
		Private service provider
		Private service provider
Social infrastructure	Solid waste, water, health, and education	Waqf
		Waqf
		Waqf
		Waqf
Accountability infrastructure.	Law enforcement, courts, prisons, and regulatory and supervisory agencies	Public service provider

Source Author

solid waste, water, health, and education service to Awqaf and barely focus on accountability infrastructure.

Determinants of Success

To achieve affordable housing and food security, it is necessary to ensure both availability and affordability: produce sustainably without unfair price formation of assets. The Islamic proposition is that providing affordable housing and assuring food security will eradicate poverty. However, to end poverty in a sustainable but not sporadic way, Hisbah enforcement of divine advice is needed to ensure that factors of production are not hijacked by a few, leading to another round of wars, financial crises, upheavals, poverty, and hence human misery. Hisbah should ensure that the system supports the genuine effort and punishes rent-seeking. It should also ensure that Taqwa and intellect, not opportunism and populism, are the norm in society. Taqwa is observing the Almighty's guidance about to-dos and not-to-dos. Muhammad (ﷺ) indicated that "all humans are equal except for Taqwa." Those communities observing the Almighty's advice shall rise, and those who ignore them, whether Muslim or non-Muslim, shall fail. No nation is the prison of its geography but its intellectual level and Taqwa. The concept of being a prisoner of geography is an unacceptable proposition from an Islamic aspect. The use of intellect, as advised in the Quran, is needed to understand divine advice.

One of the most important determinants of success in ensuring food security and providing affordable shelter to grapple with poverty is identifying Islamic lending contracts and matching resource mobilization and securitization methods. In doing so, the moral hazard observed with contemporary conventional finance can be avoided. Besides, a periodic financial crisis can be fended off.

Table 7.3 provides the list based on the reflection in the previous chapters.

The idea behind alleviating the poverty associated with inadequate food and shelter is to enhance the supply and demand for food and houses. Nevertheless, a land use policy is needed to avoid unfair price formation. Zakat plays an important role. Zakat should be administered to encourage people to own land and extract utility from it with work effort. At the same time, Zakat will discourage hoarding for speculation and rent-seeking, as shown in Table 7.4.

To inhibit land hoarding, a time limit for land ownership should be imposed so that it should respect inheritance rights while ensuring that future generations desist from a hedonic lifestyle based on entitlement to inheritance windfalls. This approach to land use policy can guide the economy in terms of which goods and services are provided by SMEs and smallholder farmers. This direction would boost employment and provide resilience against natural hazards. For instance, a natural hazard may hit an area of substantial agricultural or industrial production, negatively affecting the supply chain. An alternative Islamic version would enable every corner of the earth to become part of the supply chain. In such a system, all agricultural land will be cultivated by smallholder farmers based on the soil and water realities of their regions in a way that minimizes input use for agricultural production. To provide agricultural

Table 7.3 Lending and resource mobilization contract

	Lending contracts	Resource mobilization/securitization
Agricultural production	Salam	Mudaraba, Musharaka
Trade of agricultural commodities	Asset-backed and asset-based Murabaha	Mudaraba, 2-Step Murabaha
Real estate and economic infrastructure development—construction	Istisna	Mudaraba, Musharakah,
Social infrastructure development	Istisna	Waqf
Finished the house and finished economic infrastructure	Ijara	Sukuk Ijara

Source Author

Table 7.4 Discouraging hoarding of land

	Residential land	Commercial land	Agricultural land	Industrial land
Personal use	No Zakat based on market value	No Zakat based on market value	No Zakat based on market value	No Zakat based on market value
Rent seeking under hoarding threshold	Zakat based on income	Zakat based on income	Zakat based on outputs	Zakat based on income
Hoarding/speculation	Zakat based on market value	Zakat based on market value	Zakat based on market value	Zakat based on market value
The time limit for ownership	99 Hijra years	99 Hijra years	99 Hijra years	99 Hijra years

Source The author

and industrial production for food security and affordable housing, there is a need to change the as-is approach to infrastructure development. As-is infrastructure development is based on go-for-big, which enriches a very tiny minority, yet there is a sustainability issue. Instead, there is a need to transform infrastructure service provision based on small and flexible assets.

Moving away from the current economic and social order, which empowers a small fraction of society same like communism, should be a central discussion in the political economy field. So far, the reflection suggests that the existing economic and social order is self-destructive and that the Islamic approach is a viable alternative. The solutions proposed in this book can work under macroeconomic stability. Conventional finance practices in lending and resource mobilization/securitization markets undermine macroeconomic stability. These practices are not allowed under Islamic Shari'ah. We can restore order in our communities by robustly imposition of Shari'ah for financial management. This should start by preventing financial derivatives that lead to moral hazard, adverse selection, and macroeconomic instability. Conventional financial derivatives are not the solution, even though conventional finance seems to be based on the assumption that they are. Still, they are major perpetrators that lead to price instability and financial sector risk and inhibit lasting solutions for affordable housing and food security, and hence persistent poverty.

REFERENCES

Dost, M. (2021). *A comparison of Medina rules with the Ottoman State practice vis-à-vis Hisbe Organization* (MA Thesis, Istanbul Zaim University).

Fernández, P. (2005). Most common errors in company valuation. *Investment Management and Financial Innovations*, 2(2), 128–141.

Gundogdu, A. S. (2019). *A modern perspective of Islamic economics and finance.* Emerald Publishing.

Kallek, C. (1998). Hisbe. *Türkiye Diyanet Vakfı İslâm Ansiklopedisi (DİA)*, *XVIII*, 133. Türkiye Diyanet Vakfı.

Smith, A. (1968). *The theory of moral sentiments* (E. G. West, Ed.). Arlington House.

INDEX

A
accountability, 175, 176
Accountability infrastructure, 176, 177
Adjustable-Rate Mortgage (ARMs), 37, 52
Adjusted book value, 19
adverse selection, 28, 29, 37, 43, 149, 155, 158, 168, 179
affordability, 2, 5, 8, 11, 32, 149, 150, 177
Affordable housing, 4–6, 10, 16, 23, 24, 28, 44, 48, 53, 54, 142, 169, 177, 179, 180
African Development Bank, 130
agricultural commodities, 15, 36, 60, 78, 79, 81, 82, 87, 111, 118, 120, 123, 142, 178
agricultural land, 11, 13–15, 58, 75, 179
agricultural price, 80
airport, 152, 154, 158, 168, 176
Al-Ahbari, 1

A Loan/B Loan, 161
appraiser, 7, 8, 28, 103
articles of association, 97, 104
asset-backed, 16, 31, 40, 45, 88, 93, 95, 96, 98, 99, 105–108, 110–112, 117, 118, 120–123, 164, 167, 178
asset-backed murabaha, 94, 121
asset-backed Sukuk, 157, 165, 167
asset-based, 16, 40, 88, 90–93, 95, 106–108, 110, 117, 120, 167, 178
asset-based murabaha, 90
Asset conversion cycle, 90
asset-liability, 31, 52
Assignment of Receivables, 132
auditor, 51
autonomy, 57, 61, 80, 125

B
Bai Al-Dayn, 5, 33, 120
Bai Al-Inah, 5, 33, 47, 120

Bai' Bithaman Ajil, 38
bailout, 53, 89
Bangladesh Submarine Cable
    Company Limited (BSCCL), 163
bank guarantee, 93, 128, 129
bargaining power, 126
Basel I, 8
bid, 5, 63, 79
bill factoring, 33
Book value, 18, 19
breach, 117, 162
Building Societies/Savings and Loan
    (S&L), 47, 48
Burkina Faso, 77, 128, 132–134
business cycle, 28
by-law, 104

C
capitalist, 174, 176
capital market, 4, 28, 29, 37, 40, 49
cash crop, 75–77, 126
cash deposit, 102, 111–114, 117
cash flow, 18, 90, 130
Cash Waqf, 22, 23, 72, 157, 168
Cash Waqf Fund, 166, 167, 169
Cash Waqf Sukuk, 166, 167, 169
Central bank, 8, 46, 48, 51–53, 147
certification, 81
climate change, 60, 62, 161
Collateral, 118
collateral management, 135, 138
Collateral Management and
    Monitoring Agreement
    (CMMA), 138
Collateral Management Monitoring
    Contract (CMMC), 135, 138,
    144
collateral manager, 135
collateral risk, 118
commercial bank, 43, 46–49, 51,
    150, 155, 164

Commercial land, 14, 179
commodity exchange, 63, 79, 121
commodity(ies), 15, 20, 34, 35, 63,
    77, 80, 81, 87, 89, 93–99,
    102–105, 107, 108, 110, 111,
    113, 115, 117, 118, 120–122,
    126–128, 130–132, 134,
    137–139, 141, 162
Commodity Murabaha, 33, 35, 120,
    164
communist, 21, 76, 174, 176
Community Waqf, 24, 53, 54, 159
Compagnie Malienne pour le
    Developpement des Textiles
    (CMDT), 128
Company valuation, 18
comparative advantage, 78, 82, 148
completion risk, 31, 161
concessional loan, 167
conventional economics, 4, 58, 173
conventional finance, 4, 16, 18, 27,
    49, 53, 58, 89–91, 93, 106–108,
    119, 132, 178, 179
cooperative, 63, 64, 70, 76, 125–127,
    133, 141
Corporate Waqf, 22, 23, 69
corruption, 20, 29, 32, 52, 67, 151,
    169
Cotton, 75–77, 126–128, 132–134,
    136–142
cotton fiber, 128, 132–134, 136, 137,
    141, 143, 144
cotton price, 75, 77
Courts, 4, 156, 176, 177
credit analysis, 91, 93
creditor, 4, 33, 104, 106
credit risk, 52, 53, 88, 89, 91, 93, 95,
    119, 131
crop, 59, 62–64, 75, 77, 78, 80, 81,
    126, 132, 141, 142
cross-border, 64, 80–82, 130
crowd-funder, 50

crowdfunding, 43–46, 48, 49, 67, 157, 159, 164, 166, 167
currency mismatch, 29, 31, 32
Customs Valuation Agreement, 81
custom valuation, 81

D
dam, 78
Debt, 2–4, 17, 27, 28, 33–35, 53, 77, 90–93, 106–108, 133, 148
debtor, 4, 33, 34
default, 51, 71, 72, 105, 117, 129, 133, 138, 141, 158, 160, 161
default insurance, 37
default risk, 37, 129, 160, 161
delinting, 128
deposit, 4, 29, 32, 37, 39, 43, 45, 46, 48, 94, 106, 110, 112, 113, 117, 164, 165
deposit-collecting banks, 29, 30, 50, 51, 165
derivatives, 52, 111, 113, 118, 123
descriptive statistic, 112, 113
development waqf, 72, 73
Diminishing musharaka, 38
disbursement, 34, 90, 91, 102, 110, 117, 138, 144, 166
discounting, 18, 33, 34
Discount rate, 7
Distributed Renewables for Energy Access (DREA), 159, 164
Dividend Discount Model, 7
drainage, 53, 62, 64, 74, 76–78, 154, 176
drought, 63, 64, 161

E
East Africa, 126
economic development, 127, 129, 147

economic empowerment, 66–71, 77, 127
economic empowerment fund, 72, 73
Economic growth, 3, 4, 28, 58, 62, 148, 149
economic infrastructure, 152–158, 165, 167–169, 175–178
economies of scale, 68, 70
education, 9, 20, 22, 23, 53, 62, 66, 125, 142, 151–155, 157–159, 169, 176, 177
effective price, 136
electricity generation, 152, 154, 176
electricity transmission, 152, 154, 176
electronic Warehouse Receipt (e-WR), 81, 106, 118, 120–122
embezzlement, 46, 103
energy, 62, 153–155, 157–160, 164, 166–168, 176, 177
energy efficiency, 152, 154, 176
Environmental and Social Safeguard (ESS), 150, 161
equality, 61, 62, 155, 169
equitability, 126, 169
equity, 18, 27, 57, 58, 61, 80, 90, 97, 129
equity contribution, 162
escrow account, 131–135, 137, 139, 140, 144
Europe, 127, 163
examiner, 51
exchange bank, 121, 123
export finance, 34
export financing, 34, 88, 92, 95, 99
export receivable, 95, 98, 131, 134, 140, 142
export receivable insurance, 93, 99

F
factoring, 32–34, 59, 120, 130
faith, 119, 173, 174
FAO, 57, 80

INDEX

farm equipment, 127
farmer, 63, 71, 72, 75, 77–79, 106, 121–123, 126, 127, 132, 133, 136, 140–142
farmland, 59, 60
farm supply cooperative, 127
fertilizer, 59, 78, 127, 133, 140
financial derivatives, 126, 179
financial guarantee, 162
Financial Institution (FI), 10, 28, 32, 36, 39, 50, 52, 73, 80, 87, 91–95, 99, 102, 105–108, 111, 113, 115, 117, 118, 122, 123, 131, 133, 134, 147, 149, 161, 167, 174
financial liberalization, 29, 36, 47
financial management, 51, 149, 150, 179
financial speculator, 63, 78, 79
financial stability, 40
financier, 32–34, 88–93, 95, 97, 98, 101, 102, 104–108, 110, 111, 113, 115, 120, 130–134, 161, 164
Fiqh, 35, 117
Fi'sabilillah, 66, 151, 168
fixed-income, 165
fixed mortgage rates, 29
fixed-rate loans, 47
Fixed-Rate Mortgages (FRM), 37, 52
food availability, 79
food distribution, 58
food insecurity, 69, 77
food security, 10, 14, 16, 57–65, 67, 70, 73–80, 82, 126, 132, 142, 148, 169, 177–180
food shortage, 57, 58
Foreclosure, 4, 28
fraud, 49, 51, 96–98
freight forwarder, 96, 98, 137
Friedman, Milton, 173

Future contract, 87, 88, 106, 118, 123
future price, 123
FX, 29, 32, 37, 63, 64, 75–77, 79, 89, 95, 97, 104, 147
FX loan, 32

G

gas flaring, 152
GDP, 36, 165
Genetically Modified Organism (GMO), 77
Gharar, 43, 48–50
ginning, 127, 128, 132, 136–138, 141
ginning outturn, 136
Glass-Steagall Act, 51
global prices, 57, 89
government, 9, 10, 16, 28, 43, 44, 46, 47, 53, 67, 69, 74–77, 128, 129, 133, 151, 155, 157, 161–163, 168, 175, 176
government guarantee, 128, 129, 148
GPCs, 136, 137, 141
grading, 80, 81, 160
guarantee, 19, 22, 43, 69, 91, 102, 108, 128, 129, 131, 134, 150, 155, 161, 175

H

health, 20, 23, 27, 53, 62, 78, 101, 105, 142, 151–155, 157–159, 169, 176, 177
health care, 152, 155
hedging, 34, 52, 102, 103, 111, 113, 120
herbicide, 59
Hijri, 9, 10, 19
Hisbah, 24, 156, 174–177
Hoarding, 1–3, 6, 9–16, 18, 19, 21, 28, 32, 36, 52, 174, 178

hold-to-maturity, 50
home financing, 38, 44
hospital, 6, 16, 20, 151, 156
households, 4, 8, 27–29, 32, 38, 40, 42, 46, 47, 49, 71, 120, 155, 158, 159, 164, 174
House price, 5–8, 24, 28, 36, 37, 39, 48, 52, 53
Hukr, 22
hunger, 10, 61, 62, 66–70, 73

I
ICT first mile, 160, 162, 164
IDA, 53, 150, 151
Ihtikar, 3, 78
Ijara, 33, 36, 38, 40, 42, 47, 49, 50, 119, 157, 164, 166, 167, 178
iman, 174
IMF, 129
import financing, 88, 91, 94
inalienability, 20, 22
Indexed Mortgage (IM), 37, 52
industrial land, 14, 15
industrial production, 178, 179
inequality, 10, 20, 61, 62, 67, 69, 147–149
Infaq, 21, 22, 66, 151
inflation, 7, 19, 30, 37, 53
Information and Communications Technology (ICT), 152–158, 160–162, 164, 166, 167, 176, 177
infrastructure development, 23, 78, 142, 149, 156, 165, 169, 179
infrastructure gap, 155, 156, 165
infrastructure investment, 147–151, 155, 156, 158–161, 163–165, 168, 169
Infrastructure Prioritization Framework (IPFs), 149, 168
inheritance right, 9, 10, 21, 178
inland waterway, 152

input financing, 63, 64, 77–79, 132
insurance, 37, 42, 43, 93, 95, 96, 98, 101, 102, 105–108, 111, 118, 120, 127, 135, 141, 161, 162, 165
integrated projects, 73
interbank lending, 34, 35
International Trade Centre (ITC), 129
invoice, 81, 94, 107, 108, 110, 121
irregularities, 29, 162
irrevocability, 20, 22
irrigation, 62, 64, 65, 74, 76–78, 152–154, 176
Islamic Development Bank (IsDB), 21, 70–72, 130, 159, 163
Islamic discounting, 33, 120
Islamic finance, 4, 6, 10, 16, 31, 34, 35, 37, 40, 43, 46, 49, 52, 53, 65, 88, 90, 91, 107, 111, 117–120, 123, 128, 132, 156, 161, 162, 164, 165
Islamic mortgage, 4, 24, 49, 52, 53
Islamic Organization of Food Security (IOFS), 64, 65
Istisna, 36, 38, 42, 44, 46, 49, 50, 119, 141, 157, 161, 162, 164, 167, 178

J
Jamana Bridge, 150

K
kufr, 2, 65

L
land ownership, 6–10, 19, 29, 178
Land prices, 5–8, 11, 19
Land use policy, 13, 24, 32, 175, 178

late payment, 4, 34, 40, 50, 91, 107, 132
law enforcement, 173–177
legal risk, 96, 106, 118, 131
legal title, 102
Leveraging, 16
license, 97, 101, 120
Licensed Warehouses (LWs), 64, 81, 106, 118, 120–123, 131, 142
lien, 31, 40, 50, 87, 101, 162, 164
Liquidation value, 18
liquidity, 4, 5, 28, 31, 32, 36, 50, 52, 96, 102, 117–120, 122, 123, 142, 167
liquidity management, 119
liquidity squeeze, 28, 29
Loan, 3–5, 8, 16, 17, 29, 31–34, 37, 38, 40, 47, 51, 52, 63, 64, 68, 71, 75–77, 79, 88–91, 113, 120, 147, 148, 164
loan seeker, 33, 34, 88, 90, 91, 93–95, 98, 105, 107, 108, 111, 117, 140, 164
loss given default, 52

M
macroeconomic instability, 179
macroeconomic stability, 52, 179
Mali, 128
Management Information System (MIS), 160
Maqasid Al-Shari'ah, 119, 120
margin call, 87, 88, 107, 111, 115, 118, 122
marine insurance, 103, 105
marketing cooperative, 127
market maker, 121, 122
market price, 32, 68, 136, 162
market risk, 53
market value, 8, 11, 13–16, 18, 19, 69, 102, 137, 179
mark-to-market, 104

markup, 6, 10, 11, 41, 45, 107, 108, 110, 123, 128, 133, 136, 143
mass transit, 152, 154, 176
maturity mismatch, 4, 28, 29, 50
Maysir, 48, 49
mean, 6, 13, 15, 78, 113, 114, 129, 150, 153, 155, 160, 162
microfinance, 38, 64, 68–72, 77, 127, 164
Microfinance Institutions (MFIs), 70–73
Millennium Development Goals (MDGs), 61
mini-grid, 159, 168
misappropriation, 24, 67, 102, 111
misconduct, 103, 138, 141
modern economics, 173
monetizing, 58
monopolistic, 9, 10
moral hazard, 4, 28, 29, 37, 43, 149, 155, 158, 161, 168, 178, 179
Mortgage, 4, 5, 8, 28, 29, 31, 32, 36–40, 48, 50, 52, 53, 87, 93, 94, 108, 128
mortgage bank, 48, 49
Mortgage Lending Value, 8
Mudaraba, 36, 119, 122, 128, 132–139, 141, 142, 144, 157, 166, 167, 178
Multilateral Development Bank (MDBs), 75, 150, 151, 155, 156, 161–163
Municipal Solid Waste (MSW), 152, 154, 176
Murabaha, 31, 33, 34, 36, 38–40, 44, 46, 47, 88, 90–96, 98, 99, 105–108, 110–112, 117–123, 128, 133, 140, 157, 163, 164, 167, 178
Musharaka Real Estate Development, 30
Muslim, 47, 66, 67, 177

INDEX 187

Mustahiq, 23, 69
Mutavalli, 24
mutual guarantee fund, 43
Muzakki, 22, 23, 69

N
Narh, 9
natural gas, 152, 154, 176
Nazir, 24
Net present value (NPV), 7, 18, 149
Net worth, 2, 4, 14–16, 18
NGO, 53, 150
non-tariff barriers, 80, 81
North America, 127

O
obligor, 88, 93–99, 102, 103, 105, 106
offer, 30, 34, 63, 79, 94, 107, 167
off-grid, 157, 159, 168
off-taker, 71, 88, 92, 93, 95, 96, 98, 99, 103, 106, 131, 133, 135–137, 139
oligopolistic, 9, 10
one-size-fits-all, 155, 165
opportunism, 177
optic cable, 163
Organization of Islamic Cooperation (OIC), 37, 43, 47, 59, 63, 64, 78, 79, 119
Organization of Islamic Countries, 47, 119
Organized Tawarruq, 5, 33–35, 120, 164

P
Pareto optimum, 27, 174
Pareto optimum point, 174
Pari-Passu, 91–93
pension fund, 24, 48, 49, 165

performance risk, 43, 96, 105, 133
Periodic payment, 8
perpetuity, 7, 20, 22
pesticide, 59, 78, 140
phytosanitary, 81
political risk insurance, 123, 161
populism, 177
port, 103, 110, 137–139, 142, 148, 152, 154, 158, 160, 168, 175, 176
post-harvest, 63, 64, 78–80, 127, 128, 133, 140
post-harvest losses, 79
Poverty, 2–4, 8, 10, 16, 19, 58, 61, 65–67, 69, 70, 72, 127, 141, 148, 149, 169, 177, 178, 180
poverty alleviation, 67
Poverty Line, 2
power plant, 156, 158, 159, 168
PPP concession, 158, 160, 163, 175
pre-harvest, 132, 133, 140–142
Present value, 7
price index, 110
price instability, 179
price risk management, 107
price volatility, 63, 74–77, 87, 94, 111, 120, 123, 126
Prisons, 176, 177
private entrepreneurship, 6, 155, 156, 168
privatization, 129
probability of default, 52
procurement, 38, 128, 150, 151, 160
professional indemnity insurance, 98, 103, 138, 141
profitability, 73, 90
profit-loss sharing, 30, 31, 35, 36, 64
project appraisal, 75, 168
Property ownership, 2, 3, 20, 52
public budget, 173
public investment, 147, 159
public order, 153

Public-private partnership (PPP), 31, 157–163, 165, 167, 175

Q
Qard Hasan, 23
Quran, 9, 175, 177

R
Rabb al-Mal, 128, 133, 135, 137
railway, 148, 152, 154, 156, 175, 176
Real estate, 3, 7–11, 13–19, 21, 28–32, 36, 38, 40, 42, 45, 49, 52, 53, 72, 87, 89, 117, 129, 147, 178
real estate developer, 53
Real Estate Musharaka, 30
Real estate prices, 4, 7, 8, 11, 32, 87
regulation, 24, 29, 36, 43, 67, 82, 89, 97, 101, 106, 110, 168, 173, 175
regulatory and supervisory agencies, 156, 176, 177
reimbursement, 130
reliability, 57, 80, 150
renewable energy, 38, 159, 168
rent ceiling, 9
rent distributing, 175
rent-seeking, 8–10, 14, 19, 147, 177, 178
Rent-supporter lottery, 43, 47
repayment, 31, 34, 42, 91, 99, 101, 107, 129, 130, 134, 139, 142, 147
residential land, 15, 58
resilience, 42, 46, 168, 178
Resource-Financed Infrastructure (RFI), 156, 157
resource mobilization, 4, 24, 27–29, 35, 36, 38, 42, 45, 47, 49, 63, 72, 156, 159, 164, 165, 167, 169, 178, 179
revaluation of assets, 31
Riba, 1, 3, 33, 47–50, 68
risk and agency, 108
road, 76, 142, 148, 151, 152, 154, 156, 158, 161, 168, 175, 176
ruler, 10

S
Sadaqah, 12, 13, 21, 22, 66, 67
Sahibu's Suk, 175
Salam, 36, 132, 140–142, 144, 178
Sale and Lease back, 33
sale price, 30, 34, 37, 90, 91
sanitary, 81
Sanitary and Phytosanitary Measures, 81
sanitation, 16, 20, 23, 53, 62, 156
school, 6, 16, 20, 23, 24, 53, 151, 156
seaport, 160, 175
Secondary market, 4, 29, 42, 52, 122, 164, 167
Securitization, 4, 5, 24, 27–30, 36, 40, 42, 48–52, 164, 178, 179
security broker, 123
security margin, 111
seed, 77, 127, 128, 133, 136, 140
seedcotton, 128, 133, 136–138, 141
self-financing, 27
sell and lease back, 33
service cooperative, 127
sewage, 152, 154, 176
Shari'ah, 4, 32, 33, 35, 37, 39, 40, 47–50, 52, 71, 72, 78, 91, 108, 111, 113, 117–119, 161, 167, 179
Shari'ah compliant, 33, 35, 42, 87, 90, 91, 102, 106, 119, 123
shipment, 99, 104, 108, 110, 133, 137, 139
shipping line, 139

INDEX

short-term variable rate liability, 47
single window, 81
slave trade, 126
Small and Medium-sized Enterprises (SMEs), 19, 73, 155, 157–159, 164, 166, 178
smallholder farmer, 10, 14, 73, 75, 78, 80–82, 118, 127, 178, 179
smallholders, 14, 75, 77, 81
Smith, Adam, 173
social infrastructure, 16, 18–20, 22–24, 43, 53, 54, 69, 72, 73, 142, 152–156, 158, 159, 164, 166–169, 175–177
social safety net, 65
SOFITEX, 128, 132–141
soil, 59, 60, 75, 78–80, 179
soil degradation, 59
solar, 159
Solar Partner (SP), 166, 167
solidarity, 47, 70, 73
solid waste, 154, 157, 158, 169, 176, 177
sovereign wealth fund, 157, 165
Special Purpose Vehicle (SPV), 31
Spot price, 123
Stakeholder, 31, 168
standard and conformity assessment, 80, 106
standard and conformity assessment test, 81
standard deviation, 112, 113
State Housing Bank (SHBs), 51, 53
State housing development, 24
storage, 71, 78, 80, 99, 101–103, 105, 108, 111, 122, 126, 132, 133, 137–139, 141, 159, 168
storage cost, 123
storage insurance, 106, 135
structured finance, 128–130
Structured Trade Finance (STF), 93, 99, 128–132, 142

subprime, 28, 36, 37, 50, 52
sub-Saharan Africa, 75, 129
sufficiency, 57, 61, 80, 104, 130, 165
Sukuk, 4, 31, 33, 48–50, 52, 120, 157, 164
Sukuk Ijara, 24, 48, 49, 178
supervision, 43, 67, 106, 141, 173–175
supply chain, 79, 178
supply chain financing, 132, 142
Surety Bond, 161
sustainability, 6, 20, 22, 42, 46, 47, 49, 50, 54, 57, 61–63, 80, 130, 149, 150, 153–158, 164, 165, 174, 176, 179
Sustainable cities, 23, 43, 53, 54
Sustainable Development Goals (SDGs), 42, 44, 61
sustainable soil management system, 59
SWAP, 37
Systematic risk, 34, 37, 40, 45, 52, 53, 87

T
Takaful, 24, 48, 49, 72, 93, 105, 107, 123
Taqwa, 177
tariff, 80, 81, 97, 159, 160
Tawarruq, 35
tax, 16–18, 20, 21, 28, 33, 40, 66, 81, 92, 149, 151, 156–158, 165, 175
temporary cash Waqf, 22, 23, 69
tertiary education, 154, 176
tertiary health care, 154, 176
Theory of Investment Value, 7
the poor, 21, 57, 68, 70–72, 74, 149, 152, 165, 169, 173, 174
the rich, 74, 155, 173, 174
The Theory of Moral Sentiments, 173
trade facilitation, 81

trade finance, 33, 35, 40, 82, 87, 88, 95, 106, 111, 118, 119, 128–130
trade policy, 81
transaction cost, 123, 148
transmission line, 159, 160, 168
transport, 2, 6, 75, 99, 105, 106, 110, 128, 135–139, 142, 152–155, 157–162, 164, 165, 167, 168, 175–177
trickle-down, 5, 58
two-step Murabaha, 35, 157, 166, 167

U

Ultimate Beneficiary Owner (UBO), 15, 16, 18
under-invoicing, 81

V

value-at-risk, 8, 117
VAT, 97

W

Wakala, 92
Waqf, 16, 18–24, 53, 54, 66, 67, 69, 72, 151–153, 155, 157, 160, 164, 166, 169, 175–178
Waqf asset, 21, 22, 152, 167
Waqif, 24
warehouse, 70, 93, 95, 99, 101, 102, 108, 110, 117, 118, 120, 128, 132, 137–139, 141, 142, 144

warehouse operator, 101, 107, 118, 121, 131
Warehouse Receipt (WR), 80, 95, 102, 108, 110, 131, 134, 137–139, 141
warehouse receipt financing, 131
warehousing, 60, 79–81, 99, 101, 120, 127, 128, 142
wastewater treatment, 152, 154, 160, 176
water, 11, 16, 20, 23, 53, 59, 60, 62–64, 68, 75, 77, 78, 80, 151–160, 168, 169, 176, 177, 179
watershed, 60, 154
water treatment, 154, 176
wealth accumulation, 21
wealth inequality, 67
West Africa, 126–128, 138
white elephant, 150
wind, 1, 159
World Bank, 130, 149
WTO, 81, 82
WTO Agreement on Agriculture, 82

Z

Zakat, 1–3, 6, 8, 10–16, 18–23, 29, 32, 52, 53, 66, 67, 69, 71–74, 151, 152, 167–169, 173, 175, 178, 179
zero hunger, 61, 62
zero-sum game, 27, 71, 174

Printed in the United States
by Baker & Taylor Publisher Services